/H

D0811735

D.
Date D...rtists in
...89-1900.

21647

Oakton Community College
Morton Grove, Illinois

British Chartists in America
1839–1900

This popular cartoon, which was used repeatedly with different wording on the two books each time, bore the inscription 'CHARTISM' when it was first published in 1843. The Home Secretary, Sir James Graham, was in favour of 'snuffing out' the Chartist movement, 'every man Jack of them', but the tired old Duke was not anxious to make martyrs of them. He preferred to see the leaders quietly imprisoned or exiled—and forgotten.

Ray Boston

British Chartists in America
1839–1900

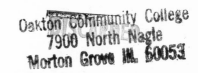

Oakton Community College
7900 North Nagle
Morton Grove IL 60053

Manchester University Press

Rowman & Littlefield, Inc., New Jersey

HD
8076
.B66
1971

© 1971 Ray Boston

All rights reserved

Published by
Manchester University Press
316–324 Oxford Road
Manchester M13 9NR

ISBN 0 7190 0465 9

USA
Rowman & Littlefield, Inc.
81 Adams Drive
Totowa
New Jersey 07512

USA ISBN 0 87471 025 1

Printed in Great Britain by
Butler and Tanner Limited
Frome and London

Contents

List of Illustrations

Foreword

There was a time when most histories of the nineteenth century mentioned Chartism only in a footnote. And there are still in use older textbooks in which it is treated merely as a foil to the Anti-Corn-Law League—to teach the lesson of the foolish, violent movement of the working classes which failed as contrasted with the wise, peaceable efforts of the middle classes which succeeded. But today no serious history of the early Victorian period can ignore the significance of Chartism. Thanks to the work in the 1930's of the pioneer historians of social and radical reform movements, the contribution of the working classes to national history became much more widely appreciated. In the past twenty years a new generation has explored the field of Chartism in fresh directions, so that we now have a substantial body of published and unpublished research and interpretation. Most of this is in articles, monographs and specialist studies of hitherto neglected regions and aspects. But there are still gaps which need to be filled.

One of these is the intriguing question of what happened to those Chartists who left the movement, either involuntarily or by choice. It has long been known that some fled to America at various times to avoid arrest and that others, disillusioned, subsequently emigrated. Ray Boston has made it his business to enquire further about those Chartists who went to the United States, and the result is the fascinating study which follows. For the first time we have some hard data on what has previously been a matter of legend and speculation. The results are important for both American and British historians. At the American end we have another little piece in the vast jig-saw puzzle of the pattern of nineteenth-century immigration history. For the British historian we have a new perspective on the original Chartist movement provided by the experiences and reflections of the emigrants

vii

21647

when their Chartist principles were tested out in the new context of American republican democracy. It is on the basis of original studies such as this that a new and definitive history of the Chartist movement will in due course be written.

J. F. C. Harrison
Professor of History
University of Sussex

Acknowledgements

Most of the research for this book was done while I was teaching at the University of Wisconsin from 1967–69. It was completed in London in 1970, with the help and guidance of Professor J. F. C. Harrison, formerly of Wisconsin, now Professor of History at the University of Sussex. I also wish to express my thanks to my brother, Brian T. Boston of H.M. Factory Inspectorate, and my brother-in-law John Horsfield, who not only read and criticized the book in typescript but also encouraged me greatly in the initial research. Most of all I am indebted to the staff of the Memorial Library, University of Wisconsin, and the Chairman of the University of Wisconsin School of Journalism, Harold Nelson, without whose co-operation the work could not have been completed in the time available to me as a Visiting Lecturer. I would also like to acknowledge with gratitude the help given to me by the following who either allowed me to quote from papers in their possession or helped me to obtain unpublished material: Mr. Michael Brook, Librarian, Minnesota Historical Society; Mr. Sidney Hartley of Huddersfield; Mrs. Frank Gees Black of Eugene, Oregon; Miss Joan Muyskens, editor, *The Annals of Iowa*; Mr. A. J. Peacock, Warden of the York Educational Settlement; The Curator of the Labadie Collection, University of Michigan General Library, Ann Arbor, Michigan; and Miss Hilda Lofthouse, Librarian, Chetham's Library, Manchester.

Ray Boston
University of Illinois
(Champaign–Urbana)

To my wife, Elizabeth

Introduction

Chartism could hardly be described as a neglected topic for study these days. Much valuable research has been carried out by many scholars, particularly during the last ten years, and most of it has been in specialized areas, the product of painstaking work on local materials. Nevertheless, there are large areas still unexplored, and they will certainly need closer examination before a full narrative history can be written doing full justice to the complexity as well as to the excitement of the subject.

One such area,[1] largely overlooked by British historians, is the United States, that 'shelter for the hunted head' and haven for 'the homeless, the tempest-tost', to which so many harassed and frustrated Chartists fled at various stages of the movement between 1839 and 1850. Apart from dismissive statements, such as 'those who emigrated became merely interesting survivals in an alien world',[2] and, 'In the US many ex-Chartists were completely assimilated but a few continued to urge Radical causes in a new setting',[3] there has been very little serious attention paid by British historians to the question of Chartist emigration, its significance as a factor in the decline of the movement and its influence overseas.

Just why this has been ignored, it is difficult to say. There are, of course, the obvious difficulties facing anyone entering this field of study, the mixed nature of the emigration, the continental size of the receiving area, and that confusing 'Englishness' prevalent in mid nineteenth-century America, which was able to absorb so many types of English immigrant almost without trace. There is also perhaps a

---

[1] Australia is another.
[2] R. Postgate, *Short History of the British Workers* (1924), p. 51.
[3] *Chartist Studies*, ed. Asa Briggs, p. 292.

psychological explanation for this studious omission: those groups in the UK who were politically and socially affected by this emigration generally felt somewhat sour towards those who had shown their dissatisfaction with their motherland by emigrating permanently, and historians who shared this attitude have shrunk from studying the emigration movement and its impact overseas, dismissing it as part of American history. In consequence, they have tended to minimize the effect of this emigration on those left behind, particularly in the field of Chartist studies.

American scholars, on the other hand, have long been engaged not only in assessing the impact of immigration on American society but also in examining the impact of American ideas on Europe. Perhaps the best examples of this kind of study, relative to English history, are those works by Rowland T. Berthoff (*British Immigrants in Industrial America, 1790–1950*, Harvard, 1953), George D. Lillibridge (*The Beacon of Freedom*, University of Pennsylvania Press, 1955) and Clifton K. Yearley (*Britons in American Labor*, Baltimore, 1957). But, while each of these studies opens up new ground in a most stimulating way, they also show the need for closer study, particularly in the area of Chartist emigration, since so much of their work begins only after the emigrants have arrived and settled in the USA. Moreover, they only concern themselves with those immigrants who actually made some positive contribution to the American scene. They are not concerned, as this study will be, to trace the lives of as many ex-Chartist emigres as can be found through English sources as well as American, and then examine their experiences in America in order to discover how these experiences affected their Chartist beliefs as well as their personal lives.

This then is primarily a study in English social history: it is an attempt to discover something about the very nature of Chartism in the light of its translation overseas and its confrontation there with a completely different climate of democratic opinion. It is also a study which, inevitably, must touch the fringes of American social history. But it does this only so far as it can help explain the reception here, and the rejection there, of 'foreign Chartists' as an alien influence. For example, it is not concerned to evaluate the part played by British labour generally in the American labour movement. But it is concerned with the impact of the American labour scene on British immigrants, and with the attempts to modify that scene by those Chartist refugees who went to the US to settle permanently during the period between 1839 and 1865.

Altogether some 70 ex-Chartists have been traced leaving the UK for the USA during this turbulent period, as well as some six others who were clearly affected by the Chartist background in which they grew up. Most of these left the UK involuntarily with the authorities hard on their heels; others left in a more leisurely manner but none the less serious and politically restless; and still others went to the US as curious visitors, tempted strongly by the 'beacon of freedom' but not enough to settle. They include prominent national leaders like George Julian Harney, George White, Peter Bussey and W. J. Linton; local leaders like William Ashton from Barnsley, William Rider from Leeds, John Campbell from Manchester, James Charlton and Thomas Ainge Devyr from Newcastle, Abram Duncan, John Fraser and James Proudfoot from Glasgow, John Stevens from Trowbridge, Christopher Tinker from Huddersfield, William Thornton from Halifax, Thomas Powell from London, John Wolstenholme from Sheffield, as well as younger and lesser lights such as M. M. Trumbull and Richard Hinton, 'fringe' Chartists such as John Francis Bray and Joseph Barker, and temporary visitors such as Feargus O'Connor, Henry Vincent, Lawrence Pitkeithly and George Holyoake.[1] The 70 total does not include such 'children of Chartism' as Andrew Carnegie, whose father William Carnegie was a most active Chartist in Dunfermline prior to the emigration of the family in 1848; and Samuel Fielden, son of a leading Todmorden Chartist, who as a result of the efforts of M. M. Trumbull, was fortunate enough to get only a life prison sentence for his part in the Chicago Haymarket riots of 1886. This study also considers, but does not include in the total, several trade unionists and a number of skilled workmen without a union who were almost certainly affected by the Chartist programme even if they were not actual Chartists.

The study consists of eight chapters: the first reviews the hopes, ideals and aspirations of the Chartists from the very beginning of the movement. The second chapter describes how Radical and Chartist leaders, responsible for propagating the misleading myth about American democracy, failed to contain the enthusiasm they aroused. Chapter Three is concerned with categorizing and estimating the numbers of Chartist emigrants to the US during the period under review. Chapter Four begins to consider the working out of Chartism in America by explaining the political disillusionment which was sooner or later expressed by nearly all Chartist refugees. Chapter Five examines the interesting and most lasting collaboration that took place between

[1] For full alphabetical list with biographical details, see Appendix A.

Chartist immigrants and those eastern workingmen involved in a Land Reform movement. Chapter Six describes some of the more unusual reactions to the Slavery issue among emigre Chartists both prior to and during the Civil War. Chapter Seven continues this investigation in order to describe the Americanization of the later Chartist aspiration towards social democracy. And in the concluding chapter a comparison of those Chartists in America with those in the UK during the same period suggests certain modifications and refinements that should now be considered regarding 'the blank in English Socialism' from 1855 to about 1895.[1]

[1] C. R. Fay, *Life and Labour in the Nineteenth Century* (Cambridge, 1920), p. 245.

I

Chartist aims
and aspirations

Liberty, such as deserves the name, is the portion of the mass of
the citizens, and not the haughty license of some predominating
faction.

Edmund Burke[1]

The movement for reform in Britain in the third decade of the nineteenth century, like the corresponding agitation in America during
these same years, attracted at first a great variety of reformers each with
his own particular brand of salvation: a stake in the land, the prohibi-
tion of alcoholic beverages, the end to capital punishment, complete
political and social equality for women.[2] But, just as the reforming zeal
in America was eventually canalized into the one general demand for
the abolition of slavery,[3] so in Britain it became focused in the six
demands for political democracy which would serve as a new Magna
Carta for Britain.

The 'Six Points' were: manhood suffrage, annual Parliaments, payment of Members of Parliament, equal electoral districts, abolition of
property qualifications for Members, and voting by secret ballot. By 1838,
these demands, together with various local grievances, had accumulated
in all but the most backward or 'feudal' parts of the country,[4] and the
snowball metaphor which James Morrison, editor of *The Pioneer*,

[1] This quotation appears just below the title on the front page of the first
issue of *The Charter*, published 27 Jan. 1839.
[2] There is more than negative significance in the fact that, 'in every 100,000
names (to the Chartist petition of 1848) there were 8,200 women' (*Hansard*, 3rd
series, vol. xcviii, p. 290) since it served as a measure of the interest in politics
which many women had begun to take.
[3] See Whitney R. Cross, *The Burned-over District* (Cornell University Press,
1950), p. 270.
[4] Chartism was strongest in the industrial north and weakest in the purely
agricultural areas. See *Chartist Studies*, ed. Asa Briggs, p. 288.

originally applied to trade unionism, had become more applicable to the new Chartist movement. 'Our little snowballs have all been rolled together and formed into a mighty avalanche. . . . The watchword now is unity of action':[1] this was how Morrison expressed himself in 1834 as the spokesman for the more ambitious of the Owenite trade unionists. He also anticipated the 'ascendant scale' ideal of the more moderate Chartists when he remarked: 'With us universal suffrage will begin in our lodges, extend to the general union, embrace the management of trade, and finally swallow up the political power.'[2]

Chartism, however, grew not just out of the disappointed hopes of Owenite trade unionists. It grew more generally out of working-class disillusionment with the Reform Bill of 1832. The realization that, 'the promoters of the Reform Bill projected it, not with a view to subvert or even to remodel our aristocratic institutions, but to consolidate them by a reinforcement of sub-aristocracy from the middle classes',[3] steeled the hearts of workingmen against any further piecemeal reform which fell short of manhood suffrage. Indeed they viewed most Radical efforts to obtain small concessions on their behalf after 1832 with positive class suspicion, as so many attempts to erect barriers against complete democracy. The favourite Radical franchise measure was household suffrage and this the Chartists opposed most strongly. Two extracts from Chartist periodicals on this issue will serve to illustrate the general Chartist attitude towards piecemeal reform:

It is plain it would be preferable to have the old Tory system revived, to any £5 or Household Suffrage. By the former we might expect to have our ranks filled with men who, rather than have no extension, would demand Universal Suffrage; while by the latter we have the gloomy prospect of increased foes, and a decreased force to overcome them.[4]

Six million non-electors could sooner wrest their rights from 800,000 electors, than four millions could from three. Indeed, we should lose support instead of gaining strength: now, great numbers of the middle class, being unenfranchised, are with us, because they want the vote—give them the vote, and having all they want—we can calculate on their support no longer.[5]

The ballot, of course, was approved of as one of the six points of the Charter: but, standing by itself, it was considered a menace, since it could and would deprive the unenfranchised masses of the indirect influence they had been accustomed to exercise at elections. They could accomplish much by cheering or groaning as the voters publicly

[1] *The Pioneer*, 22 Feb. 1834.　　　　　[2] *Ibid.*, 31 May 1834.
[3] *Poor Man's Guardian*, 25 Oct. 1832.　[4] *Chartist Circular*, 5 Sept. 1840.
[5] *Notes to the People*, p. 32.

announced their choice. Moreover, besides intimidation at the polls, the workers had another and more potent means of control over elections, namely the boycott of tradesmen who failed to please their customers by their votes. Chartists, therefore, regarded the unrestrained power of an enfranchised minority to vote as it chose, without reference to public opinion, as comparable to secret balloting in Parliament.[1] As the *Chartist Circular* put the matter:

The franchise being limited, a power was vested by law in a given number of individuals, to perform a certain duty not for their own benefit—not according to their own pleasure, but for the good of the community,— would it then be reasonable to afford these men acting as agents for others, to perform that duty secretly—to remove themselves completely from the control of those for whose interests they were, or at least ought to be, acting?[2]

The other points of the Charter were urged as much upon the basis of class interest as of democratic theory, which was based on the principles of Major John Cartwright (1740–1824), that 'firm, consistent and persevering advocate of universal suffrage and reform in Parliament'.[3] The distribution of seats in Parliament had a distinct class significance, since those boroughs and counties which were without adequate representation were the centres of large industrial populations, sure to be either Radical or Chartist. The necessity, then, for a redistribution of seats in accordance with population seemed as great, from the Chartist point of view, as the necessity for a widened suffrage.

Again, the property qualification for membership in the House of Commons, together with the absence of any remuneration for Members of Parliament, made it practically impossible for working men to secure any representation without going outside their own class for their leaders, and this they were very reluctant to do. 'Of what use,' asked William Lovett, 'is the giving me the vote and freedom of choice if I can only choose rich men?'[4] The ballot was welcomed as a protection to the poor voter from coercion by landlord or employer; but, as we have seen, Chartists cared nothing for the ballot unless it was accompanied by manhood suffrage. Annual elections were deemed necessary to keep the people's representatives from losing touch with their constituents. In short, Chartists felt that each of the six points was not only just in itself but could hardly fail to weaken the conservative forces

[1] *Bronterre's National Reformer*, 15 Jan. 1837.
[2] *Chartist Circular*, 26 Oct. 1839.
[3] Words beneath his statue in Burton Street, Bloomsbury, London, W.C.1.
[4] H. Solly, *James Woodford, Carpenter and Chartist*, 2 vols. (London, 1881). The citation is in the book's appendix and is made from a letter to the author.

dominating British politics, always provided that their programme was made law as a complete unit.

It has been said that the Chartists insisted too narrowly upon the exact terms of their Charter.[1] This may have been so at first, but when Engels claimed in 1844 that there was no longer a mere politician among the Chartists, it is difficult to bring any evidence against his statement. Undoubtedly Engels, along with Ernest Jones and G. J. Harney, was trying very hard at this stage of the movement to identify Chartism with international socialism. However, the following extract from an article by W. J. Linton does suggest that quite a few of the more moderate Chartists fell into the error of treating political power as a sufficient goal for their efforts . . . at least in the early days of the movement:

> The Chartist movement was a protest, there was no plan beyond that. Chartism . . . was the plain operation of democracy pure and simple; not republican, for it asked only popular rule without thought of organization of society. It was just a people's protest against absolutism, monarchical or oligarchical—against privilege and class legislation: a simple claim for some voice in the appointment of governors or civil servants . . . misliking secret societies or open violence, and wise enough, too, to perceive the powerlessness of conspiracy against the reigning oppression, [we] sought rather to call forth legally and peaceably such an expression of public opinion as should be sufficient of itself to obtain redress. . . . I being with these Chartists through nearly the whole of the contest, in close companionship with some of the leaders, had opportunity of knowing what they were.[2]

Such modest aims were unquestionably a long way behind those expressed by the majority of Chartists who valued the franchise more as a means for social and economic advancement. Perhaps the most familiar illustration of this point of view is from the speech of the Reverend J. R. Stephens, the Tory-Chartist, at Kersal Moor, near Manchester:

> The question of universal suffrage was, after all, a knife and fork question. If any man asked him what he meant by universal suffrage, he would tell him . . . every man had a right to have a good coat and hat, a good roof over his head, a good dinner upon his table, no more work than would keep him in health, and as much wages as would keep him in plenty, and the enjoyment of those pleasures of life which a reasonable man could desire.[3]

[1] F. Engels, *Condition of the Working Class in England in 1844* (London, 1892; reprint from 1845), p. 235.
[2] W. J. Linton, 'Who were the Chartists?' *Century Magazine*, vol. 23, p. 421.
[3] *Annual Register*, vol. lxxx (1838), p. 311.

Ernest Jones asked with equal emphasis: 'What do we want political power for, except to grant free access to all the means of labour, land and machinery?'[1]

The conservative opponents of Chartism were even more explicit about the economic aims of the movement. In the opinion of *Blackwood's Magazine*, 'What is meant, under any mystification of words we need not say here, is—one universal partition, amongst the nineteen millions in this island, of the existing property, be its nature what it may and under whatsoever tenure.'[2] A few years later this same magazine went into further details of this 'threatened' general expropriation:

Repudiation of state engagements . . . confiscation of property under the name of a graded tax; the abolition of primogeniture in order to ruin the landed interest; the issue of assignats in order to sustain the state under the shock to credit which such measures would necessarily occasion, might with confidence be looked for.[3]

Clearly the magazine exaggerated both the intentions of the Chartist leaders and their probable ability to carry their views into effect, even in a House of Commons chosen on the basis of the six points. But it was right in supposing that the mainspring of the agitation was the desire of the working classes, especially in the great industrial towns of Lancashire and Yorkshire, to improve their economic condition. To accomplish this, the Chartist leaders without exception were in favour of legislation which would tend to secure 'an equitable distribution of property', although some sought this readjustment through the abolition of existing class legislation (for example, William Lovett and John Collins[4]) while others proposed legislative programmes more or less socialistic in character, ranging from O'Brien, who was opposed to the nationalization of anything *but* land, to Jones and Harney, the leaders of the extreme collectivists of the party.

It is perhaps necessary to point out here that economic conditions were not the prime motivation for Chartists everywhere. For example, Chartism among the semi-skilled as well as the skilled workers in Newcastle, Sunderland and the surrounding areas of Northumberland and Durham, was of an entirely different nature from that in Lancashire and Yorkshire. In the north-east areas, where there was a higher level of employment and greater local unity than was the case elsewhere,

---

[1] *Notes to the People*, p. 301.
[2] *Blackwood's Magazine*, Sept. 1842, p. 53.
[3] *Ibid.*, June 1848, p. 48.
[4] Wm. Lovett and John Collins, *Chartism* (London, 1841), p. 22.

Chartists followed Radical leadership and were more concerned with politics than economics.

In December 1839, General Napier wrote to Philips of the Home Office concerning conditions in the north-east: 'It was for their political rights they were struggling and quite unconnected with the question of wages, respecting which they had no complaint to make.'[1] Thomas Devyr, a leading Chartist in Newcastle from 1838 to 1840, underlines this point in another way when he writes with some irritation that the subject of land ownership, his main preoccupation, rarely got much of a hearing at Chartist meetings because of 'the hot talk about the vote'.[2] His only recourse was to get 'hints edged into *The Liberator* now and then'.[3]

Again, turning to the question of Chartist views about national finance, it would be misleading to assume as so many contemporaries did, that because many Chartists denounced the national debt, they must be preparing to outlaw it without compensation. There was certainly considerable envy among Chartists of the cheapness of government in America.

The business of government is incomparably better executed in America than with us, and has the vast advantage of cheapness to the bargain. A vigorous-minded, active President, receives £5,200; whilst we pay to a maiden Queen of twenty or twenty-one, who is neither vigorous nor officially active, £385,000, being seventy-four times more than the former.[4]

This theme of cheap government had a most prominent place in a list of local grievances drawn up by Manchester Chartists. 'The debt that was originally borrowed has been paid off seven times over,' wrote John Campbell, secretary to the National Charter Association in 1841, 'yet we the producers have to pay this debt without ever stopping.'[5] Feargus O'Connor widened the implications somewhat in the following editorial:

Turn to America, there the United States treasury has failed, become bankrupt, and who are the first to suffer there? Why the representatives of the people who have their salaries cut while the people are not at all affected! Now treasure that up. In England there never was so much money, and so much poverty: the unrepresented starving and the represented tiring invention to find an outlay for capital and a means for its

---

[1] Quoted by W. H. Maehl from H.O. 40/53, ff. 853–54.
[2] T. A. Devyr, *The Odd Book* (Greenpoint, New York, 1882), pp. 191–92.
[3] *Ibid.*
[4] *The Charter*, 20 Oct. 1839, p. 622.
[5] J. Campbell, *An Examination of the Corn and Provision Laws* (1841), p. 62.

investment. While in America the representatives are starving and the people are not. Now, is it not plain that if your representatives were your servants instead of being your masters, and if their salaries depended upon your ability to pay them, that they would look sharply after your comfort and means ?[1]

However, although conservative fears were somewhat exaggerated, they were also understandable in view of the fact that a leading Chartist journal had expressed the hope that 'the fundholder's title to draw interest' might one day be abolished.[2] Moreover, when the Chartist 'National Petition' of 1842 was discussed in Parliament, the following paragraph caused the most comment and alarm:

Your petitioners complain that they are taxed to pay the interest of what is termed the National Debt—a debt amounting at present to eight hundred millions of pounds—being only a portion of the enormous amount expended in cruel and expensive wars for the suppression of all liberty, by men not authorized by the people, and who, consequently, had no right to tax posterity for the outrages committed by them upon mankind.[3]

The Chartists were not of course unanimous as to the proper principles of national finance. They all favoured direct as opposed to indirect taxation, and they all favoured a use of the taxing power, not only in such a way as to equalize the burden of national expenditure but also to lessen the existing inequalities in the distribution of wealth. A comparatively little-known Chartist periodical, *Power of the Pence*, put this intention with some frankness: 'In theory, a property tax is the most equitable one that could be desired. Its principles and meaning are to mulct the rich for the poor, to level wealth, and to produce social equilibrium.'[4] Ernest Jones expressed the same view in *Notes to the People*: 'Wealth [in America] is beginning to centralize. It is in its nature—all other evils follow in its wake. It should be the duty of government to counteract that centralization by laws having a distributive tendency.'[5] William Lovett, rather late in the day (1853), also praised direct taxation and favoured the absorption of the 'unearned increment' of land values.[6] James Bronterre O'Brien held that the land

[1] Signed article by O'Connor, *Northern Star*, 19 Feb. 1842, p. 1.
[2] *Chartist Circular*, 7 March 1840, p. 2.
[3] The whole text of the petition is given in *Hansard*, 3rd series, vol. xlii, pp. 1376–81.
[4] *Power of the Pence*, 23 Dec. 1848.
[5] *Notes to the People*, p. 2.
[6] W. Lovett, *Social and Political Morality* (London, 1853), p. 191.

rental 'would form a national fund adequate to defray all charges of the public service . . . without the necessity for any taxation'.[1]

O'Brien and Jones were zealous champions of the principle of co-operation, and promised their followers as well as themselves that a Parliament reformed on the basis of the Charter would subsidize co-operative industry. Their purpose would be: 'To put an end to profit-mongering—to emancipate the working classes from wage slavery, by enabling them to become their own masters; to destroy monopoly and to counteract the centralization of wealth by its equable and general diffusion.'[2] This had also been the purpose of John Francis Bray's forceful exposition of the Socialist theme of unequal exchange and demand for social justice, contained in that far-sighted book, *Labour's Wrongs and Labour's Remedy; or, the Age of Might and the Age of Right*.[3] Bray's debt to William Thompson, the co-operative Socialist, and to Robert Owen, was, like that of O'Brien and Jones, considerable. On the other hand, Bray's solution to the immediate problems of society— joint stock companies organized on a national basis—was peculiarly his own. Bray also, like O'Brien and Jones, regarded universal suffrage and its concomitants, 'not as an end, but as the means—as one step towards such organic changes as will ultimately enable the producer of wealth to receive and retain the full reward of his exertions'.[4] Unlike them, how-ever, Bray, who had been born in America and only came over to England when he was 13 years old, became impatient with the move-ment's progress and returned to the USA, largely because his book had been so poorly received by his Chartist colleagues. Ernest Jones, on the other hand, turned on his attackers in the movement to ask: 'But how would it be, if they (the co-operative producers) had political power to give them a start? If they had a House of Commons to vote them £100,000,000 sterling, levied by direct taxation on the rich?'[5]

At this point it must be admitted that by the time Ernest Jones was able to ask this question, the Chartist movement was considerably changed and almost entirely in the hands of the collectivists of which he was the leader. The earlier demand for political reform within the framework of a parliamentary ideal, a demand which grew naturally out of eighteenth-century radicalism, had grown or refined itself to the

[1] *Propositions of the National Reform League for the Peaceful Re-Generation of Society* (London, 1850), p. 8.
[2] *Notes to the People*, p. 27.
[3] First published in parts in 1838.
[4] *Leeds Times*, 2 Sept. 1837.
[5] *Notes to the People*, p. 603.

search for social democracy, a search which led some Chartists, notably Jones and Harney, into socialism. The progression was associated with a further shift in emphasis from local parochialism to international commitment and action. Both Jones and Harney looked beyond the Channel and across the Atlantic to social movements abroad: they were prepared to analyse foreign social situations, like those in France and Italy as well as in Germany and America. They were also prepared to propound a foreign policy of their own.

This changed outlook of Chartist leaders after 1848, was, of course, greatly influenced by the emigration of so many of the old Chartist rank-and-file at various stages of the movement. As we shall see when we consider the question more closely, some 'hundreds' left for a new life overseas during the 1840's, taking much of the vigour of the mass movement with them. Their departure, while it enabled those leaders who remained behind to make the most of a single appeal rather than waste their energies through double or multiple appeals, robbed the movement of its mass interest and importance.

But those who remained, and they were in the majority despite the size and influence of the group which emigrated, did not necessarily all share the new outlook. There was certainly an increased popular interest in foreign issues which led up naturally to the popular excitement just before and during the Crimean War. It also extended to the American Civil War which, even more than the Polish and Italian national movements, helped to widen the horizons of the British workers. 'America is a standing rebuke to England,' wrote E. S. Beesly in 1865. 'Her free institutions, her prosperity, the education of her people, the absence of a privileged class, are in too glaring a contrast with our own position to be forgiven.'[1] But, while there was a limited interest in further reform of the franchise after 1848, the vision of a new society lost much of its appeal and was slowly smothered by the increasing complacency of the working classes during the 1850's.

The aims and theories of Chartist leaders do not, however, suffice to illustrate the hopes, ideals and aspirations of the Chartist movement as a whole. After all, not only had the six points of the Charter been familiar to English radicals for decades, but all of the economic and social changes advocated or discussed in the Chartist press found champions before Chartism was organized and after it disappeared. J. H. Rose, for example, was of the opinion that in all probability 'the People's Charter

[1] E. S. Beesly, 'The Republican Triumph', *Bee-Hive*, 29 April 1865.

would never have been drawn up, but for the blaze of discontent caused by the exorbitant stamp duty on newspapers and by the severity of the new Poor Law of 1834',[1] and there is much contemporary evidence to confirm his view. Lord Stanhope declared in 1839 that, 'He saw, alas! too much reason to expect that, at a future and no distant period, a Radical Reformer—perhaps some Chartist—would exclaim with joy and with exultation. . . . "Without the new Poor Law we should never have had universal suffrage".'[2] Sam Kydd later wrote that 'The attempt to apply the New Poor Law of 1834 did more to sour the hearts of the labouring population (in England as a whole) than did the privations consequent on all the actual poverty of the land.'[3]

Certainly the fact that the Poor Law Commissioners set out to put the 1834 Act into operation in the north of England just at the moment that business depression was leading to unemployment of factory operatives as well as starvation among the handloom weavers, created the broadest possible front of local opposition. The Anti-Poor Law Association had pushed the factory question into the background; now it was the turn of the Anti-Poor Law movement to be absorbed. But the relationship between these two agitations is not really as simple as such an assertion implies. There were those like Francis Place on the extreme right-wing of the Chartist movement who were very far from condemning the New Poor Law.[4] Conversely, there were many stalwarts in the Anti-Poor Law movement who were just as strongly opposed to Chartism. These were mainly humanitarian Tories such as Duncombe and Parson Bull, who became greatly disturbed at the frequency with which the suffrage question erupted into their meetings. And, adding to contemporary confusion on the matter, there was Sir Edward Bulwer Lytton who expressed the view that Chartism was nothing but the Anti-Poor Law movement in another form.

There is of course a sense in which it can be said that the Chartist movement commenced not in 1836 with the promulgation of the 'Six Points', but at the moment when the Reform Bill received the Royal Assent. But the content of this renewed agitation was such that the vote itself implied 'much more', and that is why it had to be denied so strenuously. As E. P. Thompson has said: 'The vote, for the workers of

---

[1] J. H. Rose, *The Rise of Democracy* (London, 1897), p. 54.

[2] *Hansard*, 3rd series, vol. xlviii, p. 806.

[3] Sam Kydd, *The History of the Factory Movement* (London, 1857), vol. 3, p. 76.

[4] *The Northern Liberator*, 30 Dec. 1837, accused Place of being 'the very head and chief, the life and soul, of Poor Law Amendment'.

this and the next decade, was a symbol whose importance it is difficult for us to appreciate, our eyes dimmed by more than a century of the smog of "two-party" parliamentary politics. It implied, first, egalité: equality of citizenship, personal dignity, worth. "Instead of bricks and mortar and dirt, MAN ought to be represented," wrote one pamphleteer, lamenting the lot of "the miserable, so-called 'free-born' Englishman, excluded from the most valuable right that man can enjoy in political society".[1] The claim for the vote after 1832 also implied further claims:

Fig. 1. Peter Murray McDouall (1814–53)

a new way of reaching out by the working people for social control over their conditions of life and labour. Of course, at first and inevitably, the exclusion of the working class provoked a contrary rejection by them of all forms of political action. But in the post-1832 swing to general unionism, this anti-political bias was far from quietist: it was embattled, militant and even revolutionary. To the Chartists, the New Poor Law was a capitalist plot to drive them to accept cheap labour by cutting off their old alternative of poor relief. They also criticized the revised dietary of the workhouses, comparing the meagre pauper allowance with the payments to 'national out-door paupers' such as the Royal Family;[2] and they denounced the segregation of husbands and wives as a violation of the law of God. The long memories as well as the

[1] E. P. Thompson, *The Making of the English Working Class* (1963), p. 827.
[2] *The New Black List*, p. 4.

militancy of the working class at this time is shown well by this quotation from a speech made in 1841 by Peter Murray McDouall:

I would undertake to prove that the poor had a better right to such parochial relief as the old Act of Elizabeth provided, than the landlord has to his conquered estate or the grinding shopocrat to his fraud-begotten profits . . . I would go further and prove that the legislature has no more right (except the right of force) to pass such an act as the amendment act (without giving the paupers and labouring classes compensation) than it had to rifle the silversmiths of London of their plate to make coin of it.[1]

The Chartist movement, then, coinciding as it did with the arrival of the new Poor Law commissioners in the north in 1837, drew much of the force of its attack on existing conditions from the complaints of those who suffered most from the restrictions of the new system. If one cause was more important than any other in detaching the working classes who followed the Chartist banner from the general forces of middle-class Radicalism with which they had previously been associated, it was this Act and the defence of it by Radicals. How complete the alienation of the two classes was, and how much bitterness it engendered, can be seen from this signed editorial by J. Bronterre O'Brien:

What was the first act of that Reformed Parliament? The Coercion Bill for Ireland. What was the last act of the first session? The New Poor Law for England. Why did that base Parliament pass both these acts? To place the labouring classes of both countries at the feet of the rich assassins, who rob, brutalize, and enslave the populations of both. It is in the nature of things that the middle classes must be worse than any other part of the community.[2]

[1] *McDouall's Chartist and Republican Journal*, 21 Aug. 1841.
[2] *McDouall's Chartist Journal*, 31 July 1841.

2

The Chartist myth
about America

> The inhabitants of the United States are governed on the principles of Chartism, the consequence of which is that all legislature is bent towards the welfare of the many and not of the few, the interests of the ordinary people are thoroughly discussed and understood, and nothing stands in the way of their advancement.[1]

In the decade and a half following the reduction of the duty on newspapers in 1836, the eyes of British working men were turned towards the United States in greater numbers than ever before, some for political, others for religious, most for economic reasons. The explanation for this is simple enough: over and above the fact that their attention was directed there by the radical press for purely political reasons, more and more of them suddenly discovered they had friends or relatives who had emigrated to the USA during the early years of the sharp recession and almost continual depression. Except for two or three years of prosperity in the mid-'forties, most of the industrial cities from the south Midlands to southern Scotland counted their unemployed by the thousand during this period. The 'shut-down' in the cloth trade and the plight of the textile workers, was particularly critical: 'In all our large towns, Leeds, Manchester, Stockport and Liverpool, those destitute seeking employment are in their tens of thousands.'[2] There was also the extraordinary success of Mormon propaganda in industrial districts in the late 1830's. Thousands of converts were baptized in a few years, and thousands of these 'Latter-Day Saints' set sail from Liverpool to the City of Zion, many of them pushing handcarts all the way from Council Bluffs to Salt Lake City.[3]

[1] *The Charter*, 20 Oct. 1839, front-page editorial.
[2] *Manchester Guardian*, 17 Nov. 1841.
[3] Linforth, J. (editor), and Piercy, F. (engraver), *Route from Liverpool to Great Salt Lake Valley* (Liverpool: F. D. Richard, 1855). See also W. H. G. Armytage, *Heavens Below* (Oxford, 1961), part III, chapter 7.

13

The mere existence of the American nation, with its bold and radical experiment in government, had aroused the interest of working men from the 1790's onwards. Thomas Cooper, a young Bolton merchant and Unitarian, and a very able propagandist, was overcome with enthusiasm for America on the appearance of Part Two of Paine's *Rights of Man* in 1792: 'it has made me more politically mad than I ever was. It is choque [*sic*] full, crowded with good sense . . . heightened also with a profusion of libellous matter. I regard it as the very jewel of a book . . . Burke is done up for ever and ever by it.'[1] Indeed, Thomas Cooper, 'Citizen Lee', John Binns, John Gales, Daniel Isaac Eaton, and many nameless others who had to flee for their lives at the time of Pitt's repressive measures against English Jacobinism, represent the first wave of political emigration to America in the modern period—and of these only Eaton is known to have returned.[2] Later, in the post-war period of repression, there was the example of Charles Pendrill, the Jacobin shoemaker and former associate of Despard, who fled to the US in 1817, along with William Stevens, a Nottingham needlemaker also on the run for political crimes. Others of the same ilk had followed Cobbett's example earlier that same year, most of them making for Philadelphia.

For these people, 'American democracy had set off a chain reaction destined to reach far across the Atlantic into all of Europe and destroy the chains of European bondage.'[3] Again and again radical spokesmen were to note that 'the impact of American ideas was almost beyond calculation'.[4] The course of American development had proved beyond a shadow of doubt that democracy was no longer a utopian ideal—its principles 'have been submitted to a long experience . . . and the question is settled'.[5] And then, from the heart of Radical Westminster, the London Working Men's Association issued the following resounding statement: 'The Republic of America . . . is a beacon of freedom for all mankind.'[6] Here was faith indeed. Yet it was one thing to have the faith and the word to go with it, and quite another matter to be able to distribute both freely to one's countrymen. The excessive taxes put upon newspapers by the authorities had had just this point in mind—to prevent disturbing ideas and unnerving facts from reaching the mass of

[1] Quoted by F. Knight, *The Strange Case of Thomas Walker* (1957), pp. 63–64.
[2] Cooper, like John Gales, went first to Philadelphia, a popular refuge, and then to South Carolina, where he died in 1839.
[3] *Political Mag.*, Sept. 1831, p. 17.
[4] *Weekly Dispatch*, 1 Dec. 1840.
[5] *Ibid.*, 28 Oct. 1833; 5 Oct. 1834.
[6] 'Address to the Working Classes of Europe,' 26 June 1836, quoted by G. D. Lillibridge, *Beacon of Freedom* (1955), p. 5.

people. The high price of newspapers thus effectively kept them out of the hands of the poor working man, except for those they could read by waiting in line to borrow the copies bought by taverns and clubs.

A major task facing radicals, therefore, was the establishment of a free and unhampered press. They well knew that in the beginning at least, the press remained practically the only means of educating the people to democratic ideas and experiences. In America, noted William Carpenter, there were no taxes on newspapers, books or pamphlets, all of which could be sent through the mail at a trifling cost. Were newspapers permitted to circulate as freely and as widely as in the United States, he went on, the people of England would not be in the state of ignorance and helplessness that they were.[1]

The point that radicals tried to make was that there could be little improvement in social conditions until the people understood those conditions and the issues involved. If the American example proved anything at all, newspapers were instrumental in bringing about political and social improvement. And for those who might doubt this, the radical *True Sun* declared that it was the existence of a free people's press in America which made it possible for the people to maintain their interests against any domination by the wealthy.[2]

In the larger struggle, namely the democratic search for social freedom for all men, the American experience generally provided much faith, inspiration and argument. Since radicals were anti-established church, they knew that in order to destroy privilege, they had to reduce those institutions which embodied it. Holding such views, they naturally tended to be impressed by that most singular of American contributions to democracy, the separation of church and state. No radical could forget that the Constitution of the United States had decreed that there should be no laws abridging the freedom of religion for all men. And that was the way these men wanted the issue defined in England as well. Disestablishment seemed the only answer, as it had been in America. In the words of William Carpenter again: 'The most tolerant and equitable way to continue any peculiar class of Christians is, as in America, to let it support itself: to protect all denominations from insult and oppression, but to maintain none.'[3]

Again, on the question of the cheapness of government in America (cheap because its democratic spirit would not tolerate the support of

[1] *Carpenter's Political Letters and Pamphlets*, 9 Oct. 1830, p. 8.
[2] *True Sun*, 16 June 1832.
[3] *Carpenter's Political Letters*, 23 Dec. 1830, 'A Political Digest'.

privilege), statistics poured from the pens of radical leaders, often grossly exaggerated as well as fallacious, but providing good political ammunition during the agitation for reform from 1830 to 1832. Henry Hetherington, Richard Carlile, William Carpenter, William Cobbett, W. J. Fox ('Publicola' of the *Weekly Dispatch*), the *True Sun*, the *Ballot*, the National Union of the Working Classes, the National Political Union, and many others, all attacked the official diversion of the taxpayer's money into the hands of privileged classes and all pointed to America where taxes were light, governmental expense at a minimum, and all because no class gained over another. Thus were the eyes of 'intelligent workingmen' brought to bear on that 'beacon of freedom', America, in the years immediately prior to the lowering of the stamp duty on newspapers in 1836. But, from that moment on, even more newspapers were freed to carry the message, and papers like the *Northern Star* as well as the *Poor Man's Guardian*, were engaged in drawing the attention of working men up and down the land, to the enviable political condition of America, pointing in more simple and direct terms to certain aspects of that Promised Land which had rather more immediacy than religious freedom:

for those Atlantic REPUBLICANS have shown us that men can eat, and drink, and sleep, and have children and homes, and firesides, and trade, and commerce, and agriculture, and great moral and intellectual, as well as political, weight in the world, and can be religious and moral, and literary, and encourage the arts and sciences, and have pleasures and amusements, and the joys and delicacies of rational and intellectual and civilized society—and yet have NO NATIONAL DEBT and NO KING.[1]

Small wonder, therefore, that on 24 May 1840, there appeared in the pages of Bronterre O'Brien's *Southern Star*, an extraordinary and visionary answer to the frustration of disappointed Chartists, whose very impracticality illustrates the impact of America on the simplest minds of the English working classes. This solution, which sprang from the mind of one Thomas Parkin, 'a most conscientious Chartist of no little imagination', was in the form of a Memorial to the President of the United States. He humbly submitted it to the *Southern Star* for publication, prior to discussion by the Council of the Metropolitan Charter Union. In Parkin's view, if there were none in England sympathetic enough and powerful enough to help the people, let us find someone who would, and the most logical choice lay in America, of course.[2] A week later, on 7 June, the Council finally passed judgement on the

[1] *Poor Man's Guardian*, 22 Oct. 1831.   [2] See Lillibridge, *op. cit.*, pp. 43–45.

Memorial, labelling it 'useless and unwise', though, significantly enough, the vote rejecting it was tied at six-all, the chairman's adverse ballot finally deciding the matter. However, certain radical journalists, among them Bronterre O'Brien, realizing from this that they had reached the lunatic fringe with their unqualified paeans of praise about America, now began to backtrack somewhat. Articles appeared in the *Southern Star*, and later in the *Chartist Circular*, stressing for the first time that Britain was a manufacturing country while America was still an agrarian one.[1]

Unfortunately for their efforts, while the radical press was still hopeful of containing the interest aroused in the USA to its political achievements, praising them simply as an example worthy of emulation at home, the news from elsewhere that one day's labour in America was equal to three days' keep for a worker and his family, was much more attractive to hard-pressed factory operatives than political theories could ever be. Thus the workers were led into large-scale, privately financed emigration despite the active opposition to emigration displayed by most of the Chartist leaders.

By 1840, the People's Charter had made the rounds for the first time—the signatures had risen into the hundreds of thousands—and the House of Commons had brusquely rejected its consideration. The let-down of working-class hope, which had staked so much on the Charter, settled over the land like a great balloon deflated. Where were the people to turn to now? Emigration seemed the only answer and it was urged on them from every quarter: it was urged by national as well as provincial journals,[2] by trade unions as well as religious leaders,[3] and even indirectly by radical journals since they printed letters from Chartist emigres. It was also urged by such humanitarians as Archibald Prentice who, having visited America for his health, insisted that despite the large number of immigrants who were already crowding into the country,[4] workmen's wages were still 50 per cent higher and food prices one-third lower than in Britain.[5]

---

[1] *Southern Star*, 8 July 1840; *Chartist Circular*, 30 Jan. 1841.

[2] Even *The Times* swung from its imperiously anti-emigration to a mildly pro-emigration position after 1840.

[3] *The Emigrants' Penny Magazine* categorically stated that emigration helped the people and God willed it; therefore it should be entered into freely.

[4] As a result of their own private enterprise, or American promotion schemes, or home-based communal projects organized by trades unions, as well as by Utopians such as Owenites, Cabetites and Mormons.

[5] Archibald Prentice, *A Tour in the US* (London, 1848), p. 16. The influence on Chartist emigration of Temperance lecturers, many of whom were visitors from America, is also a factor to be considered here.

Denouncing emigration as the transportation of the innocent, Chartists flatly opposed it except in dire circumstances such as political persecution. As early as 1841, conservative writers expressed the fear that Chartist fanatics might watch embarkation ports and intercept and deter 'uneducated and suspicious folk' from leaving.[1] By 1843, however, when the second Chartist programme had failed and so many Chartists had been forced to flee the country, those who remained agreed reluctantly that departures might occasionally be encouraged. But they still contended that contemporary emigrants, like all socially minded Britons since the days of Tom Paine, were being forced by an unjust officialdom to leave England. They argued that emigration could only be a beneficial palliative for the individuals leaving: it would do nothing for the suffering community left behind. The back-to-the-land movement, on the other hand, whether encouraged by the landlords to give emphasis to farming and value to their lands,[2] promoted by industrialists to hold the operatives in suspended animation until they were again needed,[3] or accepted by near-peasant labourers and operatives as the last desperate resort held out by Feargus O'Connor, their only practical leader—this was strongly encouraged by Chartist leaders such as Ernest Jones, G. W. M. Reynolds and Lloyd Jones. It represented a very real alternative to emigration, especially to those who declined to exchange known misery among friends for an unknown fate among strangers.

Admittedly, after Chartist hopes were again crushed in the late 'forties, Bronterre O'Brien, publisher by this time of *The Reformer*, half-heartedly conceded emigration to be the only real salvation for depressed workmen and published discussions of the more promising emigrant societies in his journal. However, with the return from Texas of his Owenite friend and Chartist associate, John Alexander (a skilled joiner originally from Ayrshire) in the summer of 1849,[4] O'Brien reverted to the earlier Chartist policy of belittling emigration. But *The Reformer* was discontinued a few weeks later, and Chartism rapidly declined thereafter. Of course the extremists, such as Harney, also argued that the greater the wretchedness at home, the more effective

---

[1] *The Colonial Gazette* (London), no. 149, 29 Sept. 1841, p. 609.
[2] In Nottinghamshire, the Duke of Newcastle set up nearly 2,000 miners, mechanics and labourers with gardens between 1839 and 1843.
[3] The Bradford Manufacturers Relief Committee gave £500 to drain a local moor for garden agriculture in 1848.
[4] See W. S. Shepperson, *Emigration and Disenchantment* (Oklahoma, 1965), p. 77.

would be their propaganda. But this kind of class-struggle argument presupposed a working-class solidarity which just did not exist at this time. Moreover, such an attitude could not compete with the earlier and more generally accepted semi-religious, Chartist doctrine of self-help and self-improvement. Thus many artisans at this time confused private gain with individual liberty and material wealth with national greatness, largely as a result of Chartist propaganda about the glories of America.

A consequence of this confusion, as Marcus Hansen has explained, was that the majority of such emigrants, while they may have been democrats according to their understanding of American democracy, were democrats 'only in the sense that they believed the American brand of government would facilitate the acquisition of property and position and would protect them in what they had acquired.'[1] Here is the root of much disillusionment and disenchantment among British working-class emigrants to the US.

'From the incubator to maturity, the Chartist movement was reared on the American destiny,' says Dr. Lillibridge rightly.[2] But it was a very hazy and highly emotive version of what in fact was really going on in the United States. Having tried and failed to interest a wide audience in the democratic principle of religious freedom and the democratic policy of separation of church and state as it was enforced in the US, the intellectual 'prime movers' of Chartism were forced to shift their emphasis in the late 1830's to the fact of the general prosperity of the US under democratic institutions. Obviously it was a telling argument that assured the economically distressed in Britain of the material blessings which would inevitably pour forth upon the land once a democratic suffrage was obtained. And it became more than simply an effective political argument when they were able to point with triumph to the general well-being and prosperous state of the American people.

But, one cannot escape the impression that Chartist leaders, and Radicals generally,[3] wrote into the American scene something which was not really there. They fairly interpreted the American definition of happiness as primarily material in nature. But at the same time, they attributed its attainment to political democracy pure and simple, and

[1] Marcus Hansen, *The Immigrant in American History* (Harvard, 1940), p. 82.
[2] Lillibridge, *op. cit.*, p. 41.
[3] This radical assumption of the magical qualities of democratic government was for the most part held by middle-class opinion as well, prior to the Reform Bill of 1832, though even at that time certain cautious spokesmen had suggested that perhaps the inexhaustible fund of unoccupied land should be considered.

in so doing implied that happiness thus defined was a social objective. They clearly expected any democracy worthy of the name to involve a social programme of some kind. This assigned to government a role not granted to it in America. Even for President Jackson, the radical hero, government hardly carried the responsibility for the material well-being of society.[1]

In other words, a 'night-watchman' state was all that the new republic was intended to be: an embryonic 'welfare state' it certainly was not. Small wonder then that while workers left for the US in their thousands, they also came back in their hundreds if not thousands, particularly when the last remains of the popular mythology that America was unique and fundamentally different from all previous nations, was finally destroyed by the Civil War. And when they did come back, as we shall see, they came back soured and embittered as much against those at home who had sent them off with such ideas, as against American employers and America generally.

[1] See Lillibridge, *op. cit.*, pp. 55–75.

3

Chartist emigration: various categories

While politically motivated emigration clearly ante-dates the Chartist movement, it is not seen in its most ubiquitous and imperative form until the Chartist period, when 'hundreds' of active Chartists emigrated to the USA from all parts of the UK, for purely political reasons, some never to return.[1] When they left the UK and where they left from, as well as where they went to in the US is often difficult to determine exactly, if only because so many were forced by the clandestine nature of their departure to cover up their tracks. Indeed, several only revealed themselves as former Chartists some years after they had settled in the US and, being anxious to 'fit in', did not bother to describe too exactly where and whence they came. But at least some useful categorization can now be attempted, and an examination of the biographical fragments still extant for some 70 of these emigres, suggests that those categories into which this varied sample can be divided would also apply to the whole group.

First and foremost, there were those 'physical force' Chartists 'on the run', who were forced to leave the country in a hurry in order to escape possible prison sentences; second, were those like William Ashton of Barnsley, who, while not on any 'wanted list' at the time of their departure, were 'persuaded' to emigrate on secret service funds, to save the government from 'noisy and inflammatory trials'; then there were those social-democrat Chartists like Charles Keen, who emigrated voluntarily but under some local pressure; fourthly, there were those 'moral force' Chartists, many of them being also trade unionists, who were disgusted with O'Connorism and attracted by the liberal constitutions of new American states such as Iowa and Wisconsin; fifthly, there were those 'tired old men', anxious for a rest from agitation, like

---

[1] G. J. Holyoake, *Bygones Worth Remembering* (London, 1905), p. 110.

Joseph Barker, Abram Duncan and John Fraser, men more curious about than committed to the new life overseas, which was left to their children to cope with; they are in a slightly different category from those 'missionaries' like Henry Vincent and G. J. Holyoake, and those 'famous English Chartists', like Feargus O'Connor, James Burn and G. J. Harney, who were taken up briefly by the American radical press and then ignored. These last-named are best categorized as 'tourists', which they were careful to remain even when they stayed in the country as long as did G. J. Harney. But they make an interesting group, not simply because they were Chartists, but because they illustrate further the powerful pull which the myth of America exerted upon English radicals[1] right up to and just beyond the American Civil War.

From about 1825, up to and including the first few months of 1839, emigration from the UK to the USA, even from the most turbulent areas of working-class population in the north, was largely voluntary, with the exception of those organized and involuntary departures by publicly assisted paupers.[2] After 1839 however, and right up to 1848, when political persecution or official harassment of working class agitators once more became official policy (Tory reactions to Chartism being only slightly stronger than Whig[3]), there is very clear evidence of forcible emigration or flight to America for purely political reasons. The form this particular 'encouragement' took can be deduced from the following entry in *The Times*:

Emigration of Chartists—Mr. Wolstenholme, the delegate from this district (of Sheffield) to the General Convention, and Mr. Chatterton, secretary to the Working Men's Association, after being, to use the words of a correspondent, 'hunted like wild beasts for being Chartists', have made their exit to America—preferring leaving the land of their birth to dragging on a miserable life in prison, like Lovett, Collins, Martin, Fox and many more; both of them are excellent workmen and will do well having taken all their tools with them. 12 more individuals, cutters, sawsmiths, grinders, filesmiths and razorsmiths, the majority of them Chartists, are following their example. Thus then the middle class by a neglect of the interests of themselves and their workmen, are driving the

[1] The novelist, William M. Thackeray, who had declared himself 'a republican but not a Chartist' in 1840, visited the US in 1850 and delivered his famous lectures on 'The Four Georges'—as devastating an indictment of the Hanoverian Monarchy as could be found in Victorian England. (*The Letters and Private Papers of W.M.T.*, ed. G. N. Ray, 4 vols. (Harvard, 1945), I., p. 458.)
[2] Evidence in the *Report from Select Committee on Emigration from the UK* (printed HMSO, 26 May 1826), 404, IV, p. 133, showed that many parishes, from 1817 on, had furnished money from the poor rates for emigration and that most of those assisted had gone to the USA.
[3] See F. C. Mather, *Chartist Studies*, chapter 12.

trade wholesale from England to America. Wolstenholme and Chatterton sailed from Liverpool on Wednesday last.[1]

This is undoubtedly the clearest and best example of what G. J. Harney subsequently and rightly called 'political emigration' during the Chartist period.[2] Hunted like wild beasts, these local and essential Chartist leaders, or, to use the contemporary Whig terminology, 'disorderly excrescences of radicalism',[3] preferred to emigrate under pressure rather than go to prison. But they plainly did not go willingly, as is so often assumed; they were hounded, and if there was a 'beacon of freedom' beckoning to them from across the Atlantic it was obscured by the bitterness of their feelings at having to leave the land of their birth.

George Holyoake, writing in W. J. Linton's paper *The Cause of the People* in June 1848, has recorded another typical 'persecution' case, that of James Astin, 'a man widely esteemed in the neighbourhood of Padiham', near Burnley in Lancashire. Astin was first dismissed from his employ because of his opinions, religious and political, after he had led a successful pay strike. The words of his employer, a local J.P. as well as a wealthy millowner, on dismissing him were: 'To those for whom we build houses and who live under us, and whom we employ, we shall dictate what sentiments they shall hold.' Next, finding himself not only in debt to his employer but also in danger of immediate arrest following the issue of a bench warrant for his Chartist activities, he sought refuge in Liverpool while his wife had the furniture auctioned to pay his fare. Pursued to Liverpool, he managed to avoid arrest by using an assumed name. He finally arranged to board a ship under cover of darkness, leaving his neighbours and fellow Chartists, 'and Odd Fellows in particular', to make a collection for his wife and children to follow him to Boston some weeks later.[4]

Unfortunately, little more is known about these two important and clearly defined cases of political persecution at either end of the Chartist period, beyond the facts that the Sheffield group chose the one certain way to inoculate themselves from being Americanized too quickly by settling down with a group of their own townsmen in Bridgeport and Waterbury, Connecticut;[5] while James Astin is said to

[1] *The Times*, 4 Oct. 1839, p. 5, col. 5.
[2] *Newcastle Weekly Chronicle*, 6 May 1882.
[3] F. C. Mather, *Chartist Studies*, pp. 384–85.
[4] W. J. Linton and G. J. Holyoake, *The Cause Of The People, A Political History Of Nine Weeks (from May 20 to July 22, 1848)* (London, 1848), p. 42.
[5] *Northern Star*, 16 Feb. 1840. See also Constance Green, *History of Naugatuck* (New Haven, 1948), pp. 136, 171.

have moved on from Boston to the textile mill area of Fall River, Massachusetts,[1] soon after his reunion with his family.[2] It is not improbable that, like so many other Chartists in the 1850's,[3] they returned home when times were happier, prompted as much by the news of British industrial expansion in the era of the Crimean War as by American political uncertainty in the 'fifties. But the conclusion that their initial experience was shared by many other Chartists between 1839 and 1848, is inescapable.

Mr. George Lloyd, joiner, in remarking on the mean malignancy of Whig persecution, stated, that now, when the danger of physical force was gone by—when the alarmists had done their worst—would it be believed that a bench warrant had lately arrived for the apprehension of a poor Chartist friend for attending *illegal* meetings? (Name? someone shouted.) Why, for Joseph Booth; but Joseph Booth had gone across the blue waters of the Atlantic, like so many others, and by this time he breathed in a land of freedom (cheers).[4]

Thomas Devyr, talks proudly of landing in New York with 1s. 3d. in his pocket, after narrowly escaping arrest in Liverpool in 1840;[5] Peter Bussey was in a similar plight on both sides of the Atlantic;[6] while the phrase, 'made himself too conspicuous and notorious and had to leave England in a hurry',[7] occurs so often in the scraps of biographical material left by these men, that it was clearly an identifying label worn proudly for the rest of their lives, and synonymous with the general description, 'physical force' Chartist.

The case of William Ashton, however, is of special interest since it reveals something of the workings of the internal security system of the time. He was a Barnsley linen-weaver, born in Silkstone, near Barnsley, in 1806, transported in 1830 for alleged complicity in strike riots, liberated in 1838 and brought back from Australia by the subscriptions of his fellow weavers to play a leading part in the Chartist movement

---

[1] In Fall River, Ben Brierley, the Lancashire dialect writer, saw so many Lancashire lads that he wrote: 'I soon forgeet wheere I wur, and fancied I're i' England, an' wur th' only Yankee i' th' company. I towd 'em I wouldno forget 'em when I geet back to Ameriky.' (Benjamin Brierley, *Abo' th'-Yate in Yankeeland* (Manchester, 1885), p. 135.

[2] Linton and Holyoake, *op. cit.*, p. 43. See also Agnes Hannay, *A Chronicle of Industry on the Mill River* (Northampton, 1935), p. 94.

[3] See W. J. Shepperson, *Emigration and Disenchantment* (Norman, 1965) p. 25.

[4] Bolton Working Men's Association meeting, reported in *The Charter*, 13 Oct. 1839.

[5] T. A. Devyr, *op. cit.*, p. 210.

[6] William Brown, *America: A Four Years' Residence in the US and Canada*, p. 34.

[7] *Simmond's Colonial Magazine and Foreign Miscellany* (London, 1844), v. 3, p. 308.

and to suffer a further term of imprisonment before he emigrated in 1842.[1] Just before he emigrated, a report appeared in the *Northern Star*, describing a Chartist meeting held in Barnsley at which Ashton was present to hear the written reply of Feargus O'Connor to Ashton's charges that he had been irresponsible in allowing the Newport affair to take place. Whether Ashton had been supplied by *agents provocateurs* with certain information about O'Connor is not known for sure, but it can perhaps be presumed from the otherwise inexplicable over-reaction of Ashton to his old friend O'Connor's excuses:

Ashton replied, after Feargus O'Connor's letter of explanation (sent from Ireland) had been read, that O'Connor was a liar, and that he (Ashton) was now going out to America at the expense of his former persecutors and the bitter enemies of the people. He left for Liverpool the next morning.[2]

Here it would seem, is a new category of Chartist refugee, namely the remittance man, emigrating at the expense of his former persecutors, the police. There is also a suspicion that George White, O'Connor's trusty lieutenant, political agent and special reporter on the *Northern Star*, left under the same auspices. But it is no more than a reasonable guess, based on Gammage's remark that, 'White, Campbell and Mason emigrated to America (after being in the hands of the authorities) . . . all part of the vast emigration which tended to weaken the Chartist body by depriving it of its leaders.[3] Needless to say, assistance of this sort to ensure the quick and silent departure of 'embarrassing' radicals, was rendered with considerable circumspection from secret service funds. But the fact that such assistance was utilized is attested, not only by the Ashton case, but also by a Secret Service bill for passages to America submitted to the Home Office (rather more openly than hitherto) in May 1852, for the sum of £1,380.[4] There was also a long-term plan to demoralize Chartist leadership by sowing mutual distrust among them, which originated with the Duke of Wellington in 1842. Sir James Graham, the Home Secretary, quickly saw the point of the duke's proposal and wrote privately to several of the more trustworthy magistrates, urging them to spend money on obtaining information and then use this information to compromise certain of the Chartist leadership.[5]

[1] E. P. Thompson, *op. cit.*, p. 294. See also *Yorkshire Gazette*, 21 March 1840.
[2] *Northern Star*, Saturday 23 April 1842.
[3] R. G. Gammage, *History of the Chartist Movement* (London, 1894), p. 402.
[4] A. R. Schoyen, *The Chartist Challenge* (NY, 1958), p. 230.
[5] Wellington to Graham, 12 August 1842, Graham Papers, 52A.

That they did so in order to avoid unnecessarily 'noisy and inflammatory trials' which would further endanger the public peace, is clear from the actions of the magistrate, Sir William Warre, in Manchester.[1] But, since the counter-stroke which Graham relied upon most was mass arrests, we must presume that only the most vulnerable Chartists in strategic positions in the movement benefited from this type of 'public assistance' towards the cost of their emigration.

More typical of those 'on the run' and 'on their own', were Chartists like Allan Pinkerton of Glasgow, James T. Pyne of Sunderland, John (the Fifer) Rees of Newport, John Stevens of Trowbridge, William Thornton of Halifax, Mark Thompson of Newcastle, Benjamin Worswick of Clayton, Manchester, and Richard Mellor of Stockport, Cheshire—all very active and influential local leaders, 'marked' and harried by the authorities, several (like Rees, Stevens and Thornton) being forced to adopt false names in order to get on board an emigrant ship—all of these politically active working men reportedly left the UK with the greatest reluctance, without much baggage, money or prospects, but only *after* their names had been publicly proscribed and a police search was in progress.[2] They were all 'physical force' Chartists, and all did well to escape the heavy prison sentences imposed on those of their kind who were caught. Those captured included W. S. Brown, George White, William Rider, John Bates and Robert Bower, and they were only permitted to join their colleagues in the US after they had served their sentences imposed in 1848.

William S. Brown, a compositor, was the secretary of the Lanarkshire Universal Suffrage Association in 1841–42. He became secretary of the Glasgow Charter Association and was a very well-known Chartist preacher in Glasgow and district. He and David Harrower established a printing business in Glasgow which did most of the printing work required by the Chartists. In April 1848 they were arrested for printing a placard headed, 'Threatened Revolution in London'. Brown (aged 38) emigrated to Boston, Massachusetts, at the end of his prison sentence in 1850, where he like so many others was disappointed to discover that, 'Universal Suffrage is *not* producing many of the fruits pre-

---

[1] Graham to Warre, 12 August 1842, *ibid*. See also F. C. Mather in *Chartist Studies, op. cit.*, p. 389.

[2] *Chartist Studies*, p. 267, fn. 2; Lewis Masquerier, *Sociology* (New York, 1877), p. 30; *The Times*, 27 Feb. 1844; *Chartist Studies*, p. 217; B. Wilson, in J. F. C. Harrison (ed.), *Society and Politics in England, 1780–1960* (1965), p. 168. Harney Letters (Black Collection); W. Brown, *op. cit.*, p. 36; Simmonds, *op. cit.* (1844), vol. 3, p. 308.

dicted of it in the old country.' He returned home to die in the 1870's.[1]

John Rees, 'of Tredegar ironworks, mason, commonly called or known as Jack the Fifer',[2] together with David (the Tinker) Jones, also of Tredegar, were the only two of the 'commanders' of the Newport rising who escaped capture completely—or so it is generally believed. Certainly David the Tinker disappeared entirely from the scene—despite the flood of wanted posters which appeared all over Newport on the morning of 7 November 1839, offering £100 reward for news of his whereabouts. There is, however, an interesting story which appeared in *The Charter* on 16 February 1840, headed, 'Arrest of a Welsh Chartist', which could well be referring to the Tinker. It relates how 'the Welsh Chartist Jones' was seized in Waterford harbour earlier in the week, after police had boarded and searched all ships bound for America. 'It appears that Jones had taken passage in a vessel from Liverpool to New York, which, having been driven into Passage during the late gales [in the Irish Sea], he was recognized by some of the police as answering to the description given of one of the most active Chartists in the recent outbreak. . . . He is now confined in the gaol of Waterford.' Now this story, together with the report of a letter from John Rees written from America to his home asking for news of his friend the Tinker (and deemed 'newsy' enough to be reported in *The Times* on 27 February 1844), suggests that they both travelled from Liverpool together and that Rees was very nearly arrested along with his friend. Rees, however, managed somehow to reach Virginia and when he wrote home in 1844 told his friends that he had just been offered a commission as an officer in an army bound for Texas. With that, he too disappears.

Clearly such obvious refugees from political oppression, must ever be seen as a special emigrant category, separate even from those 'physical force' emigres like Charles Keen, a leading member of the Fraternal Democrats and faithful lieutenant of G. J. Harney, to the time of his (Keen's) emigration in 1849, who confessed he 'feared nothing' from the authorities. In a letter from America to the *Democratic Review*, Keen states: 'I am almost ashamed of my desertion of the cause of the Old Country. For myself, I feared nothing (from the Authorities) but I

---

[1] *Chartist Studies*, p. 281, fn. 3.; *Bradford Observer*, 18 Sept. 1869. C. K. Yearley, *Britons in American Labor* (Baltimore, 1957), pp. 32–33, 150.

[2] From a 'Wanted' poster, dated Newport, Monday 7 Nov. 1839 (Newport Central Reference Library), headed 'HIGH TREASON'.

had those about me whom I could not bear to see grow up slaves to English tyrants and moneymongers. Brighter prospects are here (in New York) for them. I hope yet to see them on the far western prairie, free as the winds of heaven, slaves to no man—neither landlord, priest nor profitmonger.'[1]

'Fearing nothing' from the authorities, Keen presumably departed voluntarily, albeit under a certain local pressure, as did so many others in 1849. He went first to New York, and from there to Kansas, which, in the late 'forties had become almost as popular a rendezvous for ex-Chartists as New York and Philadelphia had been in the late 'thirties and early 'forties. George White, William Rider, Daniel Weaver, John Rees, Richard Trevellick and Thomas Mitchell, all passed through Kansas City, where, like Keen, they paused for some months between 1848 and 1855, feeding on travellers' tales, before striking out for the West.[2]

Turning to the fourth category, those 'moral force' Chartists who were disgusted enough with O'Connorism to emigrate, the experience of Matthew Mark Trumbull, a little-known Chartist who reached some eminence in the US Army in the Civil War, is the best documented of these, and reveals his motivations more fully than, say James Dillon, the Chartist shoemaker who left Stockport, Cheshire, in 1845, for Lynn, Massachusetts;[3] Duncan Wood, who turns up in Lawrence, Massachusetts, in 1842, as an ex-Chartist emigration agent;[4] Thomas Powell, Hetherington's shopman, who took a party of 'political' emigrants to New York in 1848, en route for South America, and died some years later in Trinidad;[5] and W. J. Linton, the Chartist engraver, who also qualify here. Linton, though he did not emigrate until 1866, retired quickly from London and active work in the movement in 1848, to his home near Ravenglass in Cumberland. He was plainly completely disgusted with O'Connor long before this date. He describes him as, 'a man of probably quite honest intentions but of little fibre, and impolitic', who 'broke up the coherence and the morale of the party and . . . caused an insane attempt at insurrection in South Wales'.[6]

---

[1] *Democratic Review* (ed. G. J. Harney), April 1850—letter dated 20 Feb.
[2] *Bradford Observer*, 18 Sept. 1869.
[3] P. S. Foner, *History of the Labor Movement in the US* (1947), vol. I, p. 241.
[4] D. B. Cole, *Immigrant City* (1963), 135.
[5] W. J. Linton, *Threescore and Ten Years* (1894), pp. 86–87. Powell is thought to have been one of the organizers, together with J. A. Etzler, of the 'Tropical Emigration Society', formed to colonize Venezuela as a 'technological Utopia'. (See A. J. Peacock, *Bradford Chartism*, p. 93 (MSS.).)
[6] *Ibid.*, p. 35.

William James Linton, born 7 December 1812, in London,

was indeed a Chartist—but a Chartist and something more, as the title of his chief periodical (*The English Republic* 1851–1855) sufficiently indicates. Associated with a particular section of the Chartists, he was as regards the majority, *with* them but not *of* them. Perhaps he but imperfectly understood that the majority of the Chartists . . . fully sympathised with his ideal but held that the obtainment [*sic*] of the Charter was the first work. . . . Had he stuck to his wood engraving and left politics, he might today have been a very rich man. Now in his 79th year, he lives at Appledore Cottage, New Haven, Connecticut.[1]

However, in the writings of M. M. Trumbull, which were quite voluminous in the latter part of his life,[2] and especially in his *Articles and Discussions on the Labor Question*, published in Chicago in 1890 under the pseudonym, 'Wheelbarrow', we get perhaps the clearest picture of this moral force-type of Chartist emigrant. Born 20 December 1826, in the parish of St. Margaret in the city of Westminster, and brought up in the bricklaying trade, Trumbull was 'fighting for the overthrow of the British monarchy and the creation on its ruins of a British republic' before he was 20 years of age. It was at this stage, one day in 1844 after reading in the *Northern Star* of the liberal constitution of the new state of Wisconsin, that he was prompted to leave England for ever.

One Sunday evening (in 1846), I was at a coffeehouse in (John Street) London where the Chartists used to meet and study the *Northern Star*. The paper for that week contained a copy of the new constitution of Wisconsin, which territory was then making preparations for admission as a State into the American Union. Discussing it, one of the party said, 'Here is a land where the Charter is already law; where there is plenty of work and good wages for all; why not go there?' To me the question sounded logical . . . Shortly after that I was on board an emigrant ship a-sailing Westward, Ho!

He then explains that when O'Connor broke with Thomas Cooper after Cooper's two 'purgatorial' years in Stamford Gaol, he was so disgusted that he concluded it was time for him to take his moral force views to a new and better environment, 'and what better place than Wisconsin, where the Charter is already law?'[3]

It is perhaps relevant to mention here that, according to Professor

---

[1] G. J. Harney, writing in *The Open Court* magazine, vol. V, p. 2969 [1890]. A biographical sketch of Linton also appeared in the *English Illustrated Magazine*, April 1890, together with a line portrait.

[2] He wrote regularly for *The Open Court* magazine from 1887 to his death in 1894, being co-editor with Dr. Paul Carus.   [3] *Wheelbarrow*, *op. cit.*, p. 20.

Ray Billington, Wisconsin's constitution was a far famed marvel throughout the 1840's.

Indiana (1816), Illinois (1818), Michigan (1837)—all had liberal constitutions. But Wisconsin's outdid them all in guaranteeing unrestrained popular control: governor, legislators and even judges, were elected for short terms only; all native-born males were given the right to vote after one year's residence, and all foreign-born when agreement had been made to a simple oath of allegiance; small homesteads were exempted from seizure for debt, and married women were allowed to control their own property. Wisconsin became a state under this liberal document in 1848.[1]

Emigrating in 1846: 'it was the year of the great exodus from Ireland when I bought a steerage ticket on board the pestilential *Julius Caesar*, a worm-eaten old tub bound from Liverpool to Quebec'[2]: Trumbull walked from Montreal to Boston, and, failing to find a job, enlisted for a period of service with the US Army in Mexico. He subsequently chose to settle in Iowa where land was cheaper, rather than Wisconsin, buying a 40-acre farm near Dubuque for 50 dollars, and farming there from 1853 until he re-joined the army in 1860. But he never returned to England to stay, except for a brief visit in 1877, when he called on the editor of *The Nineteenth Century* in his capacity of 'an American General with rather eccentric views on American Aristocracy'.[3] It seems he never admitted to being an Englishman while in London, except to a few of his closest friends; and while this *could* be a mark of his bitterness, it was probably only a private joke.

Being under 21 when he first landed in the US, Trumbull was quickly Americanized in thought and deed; the same could also be said of James Dillon, who was just 21 when he landed, and hardly recognizable to an ex-Chartist friend meeting up with him again in 1859, 'except for his Chartist speeches in the local labor movement'.[4] Dillon was vice-president of the Lynn Mechanics Association by this time, and was leading a strike among the shoe workers of Lynn and Natick, Massachusetts. He had chosen the date of Washington's birthday (22 February) to open the strike, and by the end of February

---

[1] Ray Billington, *Westward Expansion* (New York, 1960), p. 308.
[2] *Wheelbarrow, op. cit.*, p. 28.
[3] *Ibid.*, p. 27. See also M. M. Trumbull, *The Trial of the Judgement, A Review of the Anarchist Case* (Chicago, 1888), p. 75. A friend and neighbour of Ulysses S. Grant in the decade before the Civil War, Trumbull rejoined the army in 1861 as a captain, was promoted to Colonel of Cavalry after the Missouri campaign of 1861, and then made Brigadier-General in 1865. He commanded the Ninth Iowa Cavalry regiment from 1863 to 1866.
[4] Unsigned letter in *The Bee-Hive*, 14 July 1860.

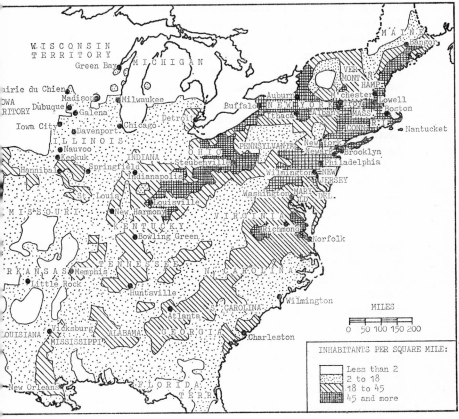

Fig. 2. The settled regions of the US, 1840

1860 close to 20,000 shoe workers were on strike in New England. The strike succeeded on 10 April when 30 manufacturers signed a written agreement advancing wages more than ten per cent. It is described by P. S. Foner as 'the greatest of America's pre-Civil War strikes'.[1]

Nothing more is known about Dillon or Duncan Wood. But of W. J. Linton, it is well-known that he retired into his engraving and book illustration at Hamden by New Haven, Connecticut, after an abortive attempt to start a British Republican colony in Montana, which, he says, 'was baulked by the financial failure of Jay Cooke and the consequent deferral of the North Pacific Railroad'.[2] Much more is known

[1] P. S. Foner, *op. cit.*, vol. 1, pp. 241–42.
[2] W. J. Linton, *op. cit.*, p. 212.

about the many Chartist visitors to the US after 1848 (the most important up to that time being Lawrence Pitkeithly in 1842). They include
G. J. Harney, G. J. Holyoake, Henry Vincent and Feargus O'Connor
himself who, more to avoid being put in an asylum than for anything
America had to offer, left hurriedly for the US in the spring of 1852 and
was treated to a great press reception in New York. Unfortunately, he
wandered into a New York store, chucked a pretty shop girl under the
chin and asked her how she would like a moustache.[1] He was noisily
ejected from the store and had to return to England in another hurry in
June, 1852.

According to W. J. Linton, Holyoake and Vincent were primarily
'self-salesmen' but they saw themselves as 'missionaries', Holyoake
being billed as 'The Last Martyr for Atheism' on the New York public
lecture circuit, and Vincent, 'The Golden Voice of Temperance'.[2] But
of rather more significance perhaps are those 'tired old men', Joseph
Barker, Abram Duncan and John Fraser. Barker, born in 1806, was
over 50 when he finally settled down on his brother's farm in Omaha,
Nebraska;[3] Abram Duncan, the Glasgow wood-turner who was
probably the best-known operative in political circles in Glasgow
throughout the 1830's, was also over 50 when he emigrated to the US;[4]
and John Fraser, the Johnstone schoolmaster who, in the initial stages
of the Chartist movement did more than any other person to create a
strong agitation in Scotland, was well over 50. He left in 1848 and returned to Johnstone in or around 1870, a wealthy and respected citizen,
having had a most successful musical lecture tour of the US. Still a
radical reformer, he received a presentation for his public services in
1872.

But, while these well-known and comparatively well-documented
Chartist exiles, some temporary, most permanent, can be easily categorized, what about the twelve cutters, saw-smiths, grinders, filesmiths,
and razorsmiths, mentioned in *The Times* on 4 October 1839? The
majority of them were Chartists, says the reporter. But how, we may
ask, did he know, and can his description be relied upon as historical
evidence? Perhaps they had indeed assured him most proudly that they
were Chartists, knowing him to be a representative of a well-known

[1] *The Times*, 26 May 1852.
[2] Linton, *ibid.*, p. 162. See also M. M. Trumbull, 'Thomas Cooper: In
Memoriam', *The Open Court*, vol. VI, p. 3348.
[3] Michael Brook, 'Joseph Barker and The People, the True Emigrant's
Guide', *Publications of the Thoresby Society*, vol. XLVI (1957–61), pp. 331–78.
[4] *Chartist Studies, op. cit.*, p. 256, fn. 1.

radical newspaper.[1] But it is more likely that he just assumed that they were Chartists, simply because they had been moved to follow the example of their local leaders. And here we encounter some of the many difficulties which have to be faced in any attempt to measure the loss to the Chartist movement through emigration. How many of those who did emigrate between 1839 and 1850 were Chartist activists or enrolled members, and not merely Chartist sympathizers?

According to Holyoake, 'hundreds' left for the US during the Chartist period, and he implies that he met many if not most of them personally, at one time or another during his many journalistic fact-finding and exhortatory lecture tours of the US between 1848 and 1890. Certainly his rough estimate seems to be the most likely, and, although he is often factually unreliable, he is more careful than most in his categorizing of who were Chartists and who were not, perhaps because he had it in mind to write a history of Chartism one day.[2] On the other hand, Julian Harney insists that 'thousands' left.[3] He too had it in mind to write a history of the movement. He also corresponded with several ex-Chartists in America while he was resident in Boston. A list of his correspondents during his stay in America (1863–88) includes G. J. Holyoake, James Charlton, M. M. Trumbull and Mark Thompson.[4] But, while Harney's most recent biographer would challenge Holyoake's sneer that Harney became 'a full-blown Tory' during his American stay, he has to admit that his friends in the town of Boston (which he never left except to visit England briefly in 1877) were mostly of the educated middle class, 'including a lawyer, a fine-book publisher and an art critic connected with the Boston Museum of Fine Arts'.[5]

Harney was obviously keener to make his enforced exile as comfortable as possible than he was to spend his energies, like Holyoake was doing, seeking out and questioning ex-Chartists. To be fair to Harney, his estimate of 'thousands' was made in a context which assumed the widest possible interpretation of the term 'Chartist'. 'Where are the armies of stalwart men that tramped over and changed the face of England forty years ago?' he asks. And his observations abroad well qualified him to answer: 'Transplanted, I fear, to other lands, cast out by England to build up Australia, New Zealand, Canada and, mainly the United States. . . . And still the cry is "Emigration!" England is to

---

[1] The story originated in the *Sheffield Iris*, a radical newspaper.
[2] G. J. Holyoake, *Bygones Worth Remembering* (London, 1905), p. 111.
[3] *Newcastle Weekly Chronicle*, 7 Oct. 1883.
[4] Harney Coll. of Mrs. Frank Lees Black.
[5] A. R. Schoyen, *op. cit.*, p. 268.

be saved by further depleting her of her best blood!'[1] These, of course, were not all political emigres: indeed very few of them were, as he well knew.[2] But he would doubtless have defended himself by saying that he was not writing history when he wrote this, but engaging in politics. He knew as well as any of his contemporaries that most of the emigration in the 1840's was voluntary and not forcible. The following extract from the life of John Buckley, radical father of Lord Buckmaster, illustrates this well enough, and is worth quoting as evidence of the solidarity among the rural working-class community surrounding the growing factory town of Northampton in the mid-1840's:

Incendiary fires became frequent in the neighborhood and this only increased the general discontent, some saying openly that a few fires would do good. Fortunately a circumstance occurred which now more than anything else changed the whole state of affairs. One of the farmers who had emigrated to America (in 1841) wrote a glowing account of the country and its prospects urging all who could to come over to Iowa. The letter was read in almost every cottage. It was read at the village inn and at the Methodist chapel every Sunday until it was nearly worn out. The Lord had now opened a door of escape. Special prayer meetings were held to know the Lord's will, which was that they should go. For several weeks nothing was thought about or talked about but going to America. The whole village was at work in packing and mending clothes. A farewell service was held in the Methodist chapel which was crowded, and the services lasted through the night till daybreak. The following evening, in the glorious springtime of May, some thirty-three men, women and children knelt down in the street, and after a short prayer meeting, marched through the village singing hymns. The whole village turned out.... 'Goodbye and God Bless You' rang out from every cottage door. Every eye was wet. Mr. Tapper leaned over the rectory gate and was visibly affected . . . news of their safe arrival and settlement (in Iowa) . . . induced others in batches of threes and fours to follow them for several years.[3]

It is, however, with Chartist emigres that this study is primarily concerned. And, while precise numbers are impossible to establish with any degree of reliability, it is at least possible to arrive at a useful general estimate by correlating certain known figures. Taking as a starting point, the pessimistic but realistic estimate of Chartist membership made by W. P. Roberts in May, 1848: 'there were not 10,000 enrolled

---

[1] *Newcastle Weekly Chronicle*, 7 Oct. 1883.

[2] According to figures compiled by R. T. Berthoff, *British Immigrants in Industrial America, 1790–1950* (Harvard, 1953), p. 5, more than a million people left the UK for the US between 1841 and 1850.

[3] J. C. Buckmaster, *A Village Politician: Life of John Buckley* (London, Allen & Unwin, 1900), chapter 3.

Plate 1

(a) Feargus O'Connor

(b) G. J. Holyoake

(c) John Francis Bray

(d) Joseph Barker

Plate 2

Bussey tombstone, Farsley (nr. Pudsey, Yorkshire) churchyard

Chartists in the country',[1] we can get some idea of the vast difference between Chartist membership and Chartist sympathizers when we compare Roberts' figure with the most conservative estimates of the crowds of demonstrators on Kennington Common on 10 April 1848.[2] On the other hand, Chartism was never a movement capable of real measurement simply in terms of subscribing members. With 2,000 members or less in 1848 (according to Schoyen), perhaps a thousand times that number had signified their adherence to the Six Points. And certainly at no time since 1842 had the National Charter Association numbered more than 2,000. (By 1850 only 500 were being carried on its books.)[3]

However, since it is this hard core of Chartist activists which the authorities were determined to break up, it is possible to arrive at some kind of general estimate of the number of those who left for the US, by comparing the total number of known Chartist arrests between 1839 and 1848, which is approximately 1,400 (i.e. arrests with convictions and a prison sentence),[4] with the lowest estimate of those Chartists who emigrated, over this same period, given by W. J. Linton as 'several hundreds'.[5]

Since the authorities had most of the enrolled Chartists marked and under surveillance throughout the period, and since they were able to arrest and imprison some 1,400, it is hardly likely that they were so inefficient that they would permit an equal number or even half that number to escape, without there being some public and 'noisy' repercussions. It is therefore probable, but no more than a guess, that we are here concerned to consider a total emigration of not much more than 500 to 600 men, most of whom were 'physical force' Chartists, and all of whom were known to have been enrolled Chartists.

[1] *Manchester Examiner*, 27 May 1848.
[2] *The Times* estimated 150,000, which included special constables.
[3] Schoyen, *op. cit.*, p. 199.
[4] *Annual Register*, 1840, 1842 and 1848: see also W. J. Linton, *op. cit.*, pp. 36–37.
[5] Letter to G. J. Harney, June 1866, postmarked 'New York', from W. J. Linton: Harney Coll. of Mrs. Frank Lees Black, Eugene, Oregon.

4

Political
disillusionment

> Universal Suffrage is *not* producing (here in the U.S.A.) many
> of the fruits predicted of it in the Old Country.

> W. S. Brown, Chartist preacher from Glasgow

The Chartist assumption, widely held even among well-read, middle-class radicals like John Stuart Mill, that American prosperity and happiness were simply the natural consequences of her democratic institutions,[1] was, as we have seen, a most important part of the Chartist case against privilege in Britain.[2] But it was a totally misleading assumption and one that was bound to end in political disillusion for those who put real faith in it, as did hundreds of Chartist emigrants to the US in the late 'thirties and 'forties. Nevertheless, it was an assumption that was clung to most stubbornly for obvious political reasons, by the radical leadership in Britain from the 1830's right through to the late 1860's, despite the evidence to the contrary and despite the loud complaints issuing from returned emigrants who made it clear that they were as angry with those at home who had sent them off with such romantic notions, as they were with American employers and America generally.

As early as 1823, the *Quarterly Review* had suggested that the vast, unpeopled regions of the American frontier served not only as a safety valve for American institutions, but also as the source of American advantage and strength.[3] But this sort of theorizing by 'mere armchair travellers' was quickly discounted by radicals as conservative propaganda, despite the corroborative evidence of the map-makers and the

---

[1] J. S. Mill, *On Representative Government* (1861), pp. 156–57.
[2] See Chapter 2, p. 19.
[3] *Quarterly Review*, vol. 30 (Oct. 1823), pp. 25–28.

explorers that America was even bigger and richer than had been imagined hitherto. They knew (they told themselves) that the liberty of America was universal in character, as much a birthright of Englishmen as Americans, and the ingredients out of which it was moulded were as plentiful on English ground as they were in the United States. The Americans had simply paved the way, that was all: had shown that when the people were free and properly represented, then 'the laws, being made by the representatives of all, are intended for the good of all'.[1] In short, it was revolutionary America, agrarian America, the democratic America of Tom Paine's writings—and not the expanding Jacksonian America of the 1830's, that English radicals believed 'constituted the best precedent and guide to the oppressed and enslaved people of England in their struggle for the Right of Representation For Every Man'.[2] It is here, then, in eighteenth-century America, that the misleading Chartist assumption is rooted, and when we look at the writings of Thomas Brothers we can see very clearly how an emotional radical such as he was, could be unbalanced by the disparity between the actual conditions in America and those he had been led to expect.

Emigration to the United States had been the dream of Brothers since his boyhood in Warwickshire, when an enthusiastic reading of the *Rights of Man* had convinced him that an aristocratic system of government was responsible for the grinding poverty that was increasingly prevalent in his native land. By the time he had departed for Philadelphia in 1824, he had come to regard the capitalist system's financial operations, in addition to aristocracy, as the root causes of social misery. In the 'far-famed republic', therefore, he sought not only to make his fortune but also to find the embodiment of his political and social ideals.[3] Shocked to discover on arrival that American freedom led to lynchings, stabbings and shootings, Brothers at first retired into himself and settled down to the business of making a living as a hatmaker. Then he began to dabble in reform activities, and in 1835 began publication of a weekly journal, *The Radical Reformer and Working Man's Advocate*. By this time Brothers was a confirmed champion of the emerging labour movement in Philadelphia, and his journal was the unofficial mouthpiece.[4] The journal was dominated by Brothers' own

[1] *Poor Man's Guardian*, 17 Dec. 1831.
[2] *Ibid.*, 8 Oct. 1831.
[3] Thomas Brothers, *The United States of North America as They Really Are: Not as they are Generally Described: being a Cure for Radicalism* (London, 1840), pp. 3–4, 11.
[4] See Edward Pessen, 'Thomas Brothers, Anti-Capitalist Employer', *Pennsylvania History*, vol. XXIV (Oct. 1957), p. 323.

writings. During this period, too, his ideas were not simply pro-labour but extremely violent, taking the form often-times of diatribes against the social order, which culminated in a most violent issue following his business failure in 1837. When he finally returned to England in 1838, he had become a firm critic of democracy '. . . and was most reluctantly obliged to acknowledge the fallacy of self-government, believing that it had . . . no existence in the nature of things'.[1]

Clearly his American experience had completely undermined his belief in political reform, though it had left his sympathy for the under-privileged unaffected. Anxious to warn Chartists, above all others, 'to avoid the United States whatever other way they steer',[2] Brothers rapidly completed his lengthy treatise on America and at once revealed that disillusion had transformed this agitator for the rights of workers into a champion of reform through aristocratic benevolence. The change was signalled in 1840 with the publication of his *The United States of North America as They Really Are*, a book which mingles some very bitter comment on social inequality with abject subservience to political toryism. It is primarily a source book of glaring social evils, for with much zeal, Brothers had collected materials on cruelty in American prisons, atrocities against slaves and abolitionists, the general deterioration of manners in society, the duplicity of politicians and the suffering of the poor. They were to document his new thesis that democracy was at bottom a fraud. But they were also to serve as a warning to Chartists of the state of things in contemporary America. 'Democratic opportunists, promising all things, will tell you (Chartists) as many flattering tales as a simpering bawd would: their motive, like hers, would be to plunder you to the utmost extent.'[3] Politics in a democracy, he continues, is full of sound and fury, signifying nothing of importance to the labouring poor. Rather than depend on themselves or on hypocritical politicians, he now advised workers to place their faith in God and in the ancient class of aristocrats.[4] Like several other radicals who followed him, Brothers' American experience ended his dream that democratic politics was the path to reform: but, unlike them, he did not come to believe in independent workers' action. Instead, he retreated to a position that would place responsibility for society's welfare in the hands of the patricians.

A similar type of confused conservatism was expressed by Peter Bussey towards the end of his first ten years as an emigre in New York

[1] Brothers, *op. cit.*, p. 2. [2] *Ibid.*, p. 149.
[3] *Ibid.*, p. 224. [4] *Ibid.*, pp. 52–53.

State and Massachusetts. Bussey, a leading 'physical force' Chartist in the conspiracies of 1839 and a Bradford inn-keeper, fled to America after the collapse of the insurrectionary movement in November 1839.[1] Joining forces in New York with a fellow Chartist, Benjamin Worswick of Clayton, Manchester, he opened an Emigrant Boarding House at 2 Front Street, close to the starting point of the steamboats for the Western States.[2]

Fig. 3. Peter Bussey (1805–69)

In February 1841, Bussey wrote to the *Northern Star* saying that he had been pleased to put up one or two West Riding Chartists who had arrived in America (one robbed him), but he offered no justification of why he had gone there himself.[3] By 1842, Bussey's partner was John Rewcastle, a Chartist druggist from Newcastle upon Tyne, who had just managed to escape arrest in Liverpool, along with his Chartist friend and travelling companion, Thomas Ainge Devyr.[4]

The next reference to Bussey in America is by Lawrence Pitkeithly of Huddersfield, who 'had undertaken a voyage to the UNITED STATES OF AMERICA, to see with his own eyes, and judge for himself as to the truth or falsehood of the very many representations that have been made to

[1] Julius West, *A History of the Chartist Movement* (London, 1920), p. 191.
[2] *Northern Star*, 6 June 1840.
[3] *Ibid.*, 20 Feb. 1841.
[4] *Ibid.*, 28 May 1842.

induce emigration to that corner of the world'.[1] Pitkeithly was the leader of the anti-Poor Law movement in the neighbourhood of Huddersfield and was hustings candidate for the West Riding of Yorkshire in 1841, as well as being a member of the Chartist Conventions of 1839 and 1842. He arrived in New York on 6 August, 1842, and immediately sought out his old friend Peter Bussey.

'I found that Peter had left New York and gone to live upon a farm in New Jersey. I therefore ordered the man to drive to Mr. Rewcastle's, at No. 17 in the same street.'[2] Pitkeithly knew Rewcastle well and therefore it is very probable that he also knew Devyr, the ex-Chartist journalist and agitator from Newcastle upon Tyne, now firmly settled in New York, whose oldest daughter, Cecelia, was a member of the Shaker community of New Lebanon, which was Pitkeithly's next place of call. He then went on to visit Bussey's old partner, Worswick, at whose house he found letters from Bussey awaiting him. On the following day, 'having received a most pressing letter from Mr. Bussey, and having some business to transact', he took the steamer to Elizabeth Town, New Jersey, 17 miles away, where he found Bussey farming, apparently prosperously. Sadly, none of their conversation is recorded, but it is very probable that Bussey expressed the same sort of impatience with American democracy as that described by Dr. John Smyles (cousin to the famous Samuel Smiles), another old friend and radical now living in New York, in a long letter to Pitkeithly prior to his visit:

This country, or rather a residence in this country of some years, often changes the political opinions of old country radicals. One sees so little of real practical republicanism that some are apt to become disgusted, and because of a little disappointment, almost become tory. But to my mind, this is but a skin-deep view of things. A people just set up for themselves on a new principle, cannot act with perfect wisdom at once. It would be absurd to expect it; but so long as they possess sufficient intelligence to retain in their own hands the power of change, time will correct the many abuses that have crept into their legislation. . . . Without a thorough understanding of what it [American government] is, I look upon the mere right of suffrage and the ballot as of small amount, and probably of doubtful good.[3]

Dr. Smyles was, admittedly, rather comfortably situated on his own estate in Rochester, NY, when he wrote this, and perhaps more kindly disposed towards American democracy than Bussey. Even so, the fact that they were mutual friends of Pitkeithly and were both visited by

[1] *Northern Star*, 1 April 1843.
[2] *Ibid.*, April 29 1843.
[3] Dr. John Smyles, *A Letter to Mr. Pitkethly* (London, 1842), p. 2.

him, without further comment during the same short period, suggests that Bussey, while possibly a little impatient, was still favourably disposed towards America at this time. Pitkeithly again mentions Bussey in his subsequent articles in the *Northern Star*, as one of the last people to see and speak to him before he embarked for home.[1] Bussey, for his part, moved back into the city of New York fairly soon after this period of farming in New Jersey, because the *Northern Star* of 30 September 1843 carried an advertisement headed: 'Peter Bussey *in New York Again* offering board and lodging, and advice about the country.' He is then reported by William Brown, an ex-Chartist clothier friend from Leeds, as saying at this time: 'This government is not what it is cracked up to be, and I believe if I were to go back to England with my present experience, I should then become as great an advocate for Tory measures as ever I was for those of the Chartists.'[2] According to Brown, Bussey failed in his farming venture and returned to New York to open a tavern. This in turn failed, and, 'four years after our first meeting', which would be in 1848, Brown saw him hawking a barrow of 'wretched gewgaws' in Chatham Street, New York, 'bawling out at the full pitch of his voice, "Any article on this 'ere tray for three cents, now is the time, ladies and gentlemen". . . nothing but his voice reminded me of the great Bradford Chartist orator.'[3]

There are two more pieces of evidence to be reported. In a brief newspaper article written by one John Schofield of Bradford in November 1895,[4] Bussey is said to have returned to Bradford in 1854. 'Patriotism and love of country was inherent in him and on again sighting the white cliffs of Albion, he exclaimed . . ."England with all thy faults I love thee still!" He afterwards went to reside at Horsforth, and was landlord of the Fleece Inn there. He died September 11th, 1869, and was interred in Farsley Church Yard.' According to the second piece of evidence, a copy of the inscription on the Bussey family tomb in Farsley,[5] 'Peter Bussey, who died Sep. 11th 1869, aged 64 years. *He was a citizen of the United States of America.*' This could suggest that Bussey was proud to have been in America, and that he had been ready to spend the rest of his life there, if luck had been with him. On the other hand, the fact that he spent most of his American stay in the immediate

---

[1] *Northern Star*, 24 June 1843.
[2] William Brown, *America: Four Years' Residence in the United States and Canada* (Leeds, privately published, 1849), p. 42.
[3] *Ibid.*
[4] Chartist Papers, Bradford Reference Library, Empsall Collection, case no 36.
[5] I am indebted to Mr. M. Brook of St. Paul, Minnesota, for this copy.

neighbourhood of English working men, most of whom were ex-Chartists like himself, suggests he wished to keep himself insulated against Americanization, and viewed his stay as a purely temporary one. His disillusionment with the New World should, therefore, be seen as little more than a continuation of his dissatisfaction with the Old and with life in general. He was probably not as profoundly disturbed by his experience as Brothers before him, or John Alexander after him; also he was not as unstable a personality as these two and not as expectant of an ideal state. John Alexander, for example, who sailed from London for the new state of Texas in October 1848, concluded very quickly that American democracy fell far short of its billing. The following spring, while living in Houston, he penned a series of letters to his friend and editor, Bronterre O'Brien, which reflect his extreme frustration with the South-west and point up his disgust with American institutions.

As a member of the North Texas Colonization Company, Alexander was disenchanted long before he reached New Orleans, by the ignorance and the pathetic expectations of his radical shipmates. 'Chartists on board "The Henry",' he reported, 'contended that the right to vote created a political democracy and thereby freedom, but their American experiences almost universally convinced them of their error.'[1] After four months in Texas, Alexander informed his friend O'Brien: 'I have invariably found that those who boasted most of the advantages to be obtained in America, were soonest disheartened and the first to wish to be returned to England.' The peculiar complacency of Americans and their acceptance of the system, with its injustices, made improvement more difficult and more unlikely than in England. 'I expected to find America a few degrees better than England,' he wrote, 'but it is not—it is worse; it is, in fact, in a hopeless condition as regards either moral, political or intellectual progression.'[2]

There were, of course, many other minor irritations, but the truly disturbing discovery for Alexander was the American failure to understand the meaning of freedom. He and others who disagreed with the prevailing attitudes on slavery, religion, government and social organization, soon discovered that they were not merely forced to remain silent but were actively pressed into offering nominal approval of the offensive institutions. In short, five months in the United States convinced Alexander that neither the political 'bobbles', as he called them,

---

[1] *The Reformer*, 26 May 1849, no. 5, p. 35.
[2] *Ibid.*, p. 34.

of republicanism nor the economic wealth of the country had effected a true reformation. America most certainly possessed what English radicals sought: manhood suffrage, no property qualification for voting, payment of members of Congress, and equal constituencies, yet the country was noticeably less free than Britain.

Here then was the root of disillusion: caused, in the main, by a general misunderstanding of, not by misinformation about, the nature of American democracy. 'Democracy does not mean equality of conditions, physical or mental, or equality as to property. It does mean political equality and the equality of opportunity.' Thus spoke Andrew Carnegie, strange 'child of Chartism',[1] addressing the Radical Association of his native town, Dunfermline, when he rather quixotically attempted to carry the old war of Chartism back to Britain from Pittsburgh in 1886. He puts his finger unerringly on the most important point of difference here. Like many other former radicals, he found it difficult (but not ultimately impossible) to reconcile plutocracy with democracy. But he remained guilt-ridden for the rest of his successful life.

Disillusioned radicals like Peter Bussey and Thomas Brothers returned home to become arch-conservatives, whereas the John Alexander-type concluded that only through a communistic reorganization of society could America (and mankind) be saved. These, of course, were the extremists. But even those like Charles Keen, the social democrat friend of Julian Harney who had nothing but praise for American institutions, and Joseph Barker who was fully aware that the USA had its faults, were perturbed by the disparity between the Chartist-propagated myth of American democracy, and the harsh reality which all Chartists faced in the urban areas where they arrived and settled. Only those emigres who kept their personal sights permanently trained 'on the far western prairie' like Keen, remained happy for long, since even the most amateur agriculturist could make some attempt to create his own perfect Little England out there on the frontier. The city worker, on the other hand, (and he was in the majority among Chartist emigres) with some real pride in his special skills, was forced to seek employment, to conform to unfamiliar standards of labour, and to adjust to a new environment, simultaneously.

Small wonder then that a temporary financial depression, or prolonged difficulty in finding suitable employment, or the failure of a

[1] See J. F. Wall, 'Andrew Carnegie: Child of Chartism' in *History 4* (A Meridian Periodical, pub. by The World Pub. Co., 1961), p. 164.

small enterprise, or even just the unsympathetic 'labour ideology' of the American business community, sparked off the return of large numbers of urban worker-refugees during the late 1840's, among whom were some of the keenest Chartists.[1] Only those, like John Campbell, T. A. Devyr and J. F. Bray, whose missionary zeal made them keen enough to warn the American worker of his imminent danger, and strong enough to find the means for their own economic survival at the same time, stayed. In this way and for these reasons, a few of the more dynamic and class-conscious Chartist emigres actively joined the emerging American labour movement and helped to convince even the most conservative American worker that he was being exploited. Most mechanics from England turned to industrial action, to unions and to strikes. Others, like Devyr, concentrated on the land question. With a frontier of unsettled land to go at, the Natural Reformers led by Devyr and Evans started a movement which was eventually to influence national policy. Out of all the elements seething in the radical crucible, it is significant that the ultimate hard residue should have been a land policy.

[1] See W. J. Shepperson, *British Emigration to North America* (Oxford, 1957), p. 82.

5

Chartists and land reform

It has been said with some truth that the collapse of Chartism, the failure of revolutionary tactics on the Continent, and the rise of 'common sense' or new model unionism in England, so conditioned the outlook of immigrant labour leaders and organizers *before* they emigrated that they became one of the most moderate elements in the American labour movement during the mid-nineteenth century.[1] Certainly, by contrast with the violent character of certain of the German immigrant agitators who arrived in the US after 1848, this is true enough. For many British working men, the ocean passage did not fundamentally alter what environment had already firmly set. Generally speaking, British trade unionists in American labour, most of whom were highly skilled and therefore highly esteemed, did tend to reflect middle-class values and it was largely the hope of emulating this class further that had prompted most of them to cross the ocean in the first place.

But there is a danger here of producing a group caricature almost as overdrawn and as misleading as the well-known portrait of frenzied, unbalanced demagogues presented to the nineteenth-century American public by the conservative press. The truth is that while the American environment does seem to have encouraged a certain conservatism in many British trade unionists, particularly in those who emigrated in the 1850's, it was often of a purely tactical kind extracted from lessons learned at home after the collapse of Chartism. One of the best documented examples of this is to be found in the career of John Siney, the Lancashire cotton operative and brickmaker who became the first president of the Miners' National Association of the USA from 1873 to 1876.[2] As he himself said on one occasion:

[1] Clifton K. Yearley, *Britons in American Labor* (Baltimore, 1957), pp. 89–90.
[2] See Charles E. Killeen's unpublished Ph.D. thesis (University of Wisconsin, 1942), *John Siney: The Pioneer in American Industrial Unionism and Government.*

We have been called 'agitators', we have been called 'demagogues', because we have counselled the members of this organization to try and secure those objects. In some places even the clergy have placed their anathema upon the society, and why? Is it wrong to teach men to seek a higher moral standard? If so, let them vacate the pulpits. Is it wrong to cultivate the intellect and inculcate broader and more comprehensive views than we now have? If so, let the newspapers close their offices or refrain from using the epithets of 'ignorant' at us. Is it wrong to advance our financial interests? If so, let those who operate our mines and our mills and all others, abandon the various enterprises in which they are engaged in pursuit of wealth. It appears to me that that which if advised by the church, by the press or by the wealthy would be applauded to the heavens, when counselled and advised by working men, consigns them to perdition or ranks them in the catalogue of agitators, demagogues and mischief makers.[1]

However, this does not mean that the conservative press portrait was based upon nothing but their fevered imagination. It was not only Moses Beach, the editor of the conservative *New York Sun*, who lumped together Eastern Anti-Renters and National Reformers as 'neither more nor less than English Chartists transported to this country'.[2] His opinion was shared generally by American textile manufacturers in New England and mine owners in Pennsylvania, for whom the impression that Britons were invariably the instigators of labour unrest, had been well and truly established by the end of the 1830's.[3] Far from being the conservative, self-centred and self-seeking money-grubbers that Professor Yearley suggests, certain ex-Chartist immigrants at least were sufficiently altruistic to view their struggle for the good life within the framework of an international trend towards social democracy. John Francis Bray, for example, made it clear even before he left Britain: 'On the broad principles of equal rights will Labour now take its stand —not Labour in the United Kingdom only, but in France and the United States, and the world at large.'[4] He and his Chartist confrères reasoned that the survival of their cause might well be contingent upon its becoming as widespread as the forces opposing it. 'Men of America, wake up! Or you'll be murdered while you are sleeping,' shouted Thomas Devyr shortly after he had arrived in the USA in 1840.[5]

Full, therefore, of missionary zeal that sprang from moral conviction

---

[1] *Miners' National Record*, November 1874, p. 2.
[2] Quoted by T. A. Devyr, *The Odd Book of the 19th Century*, part II, p. 139.
[3] See 'The Social History of an American Depression, 1837–43' by Samuel Rezneck, *American Hist. Rev.*, vol. 40, pp. 662–87.
[4] J. F. Bray, *Labour's Wrongs and Labour's Remedy* (Leeds, 1839), p. 13.
[5] *Odd Book, op. cit.*, part II, p. 150.

as much as from economic and political oppression, these 'activists' willingly shouldered the American working man's 'burden'. They also persisted in this endeavour long after it had become painfully clear to them that even Republican institutions were providing inadequate insurance against 'wage slavery'.

Politics is gambling direct. The public spoils are the faro bank, the whole nation is a 'hell', and every politician is a player. . . . And the unnatural pressures put upon the wage worker tend to undermine even his honest manhood. . . . To remedy all this turn your back on the examples set us by England . . . it is because we have followed her accurst example that all our existing evils have fallen upon us. Civilization we must have. It is part of the Supreme Plan. Shall we accept British Civilization, springing out of the ages of ignorance, rapine and murder ? Or shall we adopt an American Civilization, founded on the teachings of Christ and sublime traditions of the Republic ?[1]

The point here is that to a surprising extent most British emigre-workers with any political sense at all appear to have realized most plainly that capitalism, industrialism and the train of problems that came in their wake were western, not narrowly national, phenomena; and Chartist 'thinkers' such as J. F. Bray, G. J. Harney and Ernest Jones hammered this intelligence home as forcefully as possible to their American brothers. Whenever freedom was on trial in America during the 'forties and 'fifties, ex-Chartists joined with other reforming elements in American society, as its champions; moreover they joined with their eyes wide open. As Joseph Barker (1806–75) wrote in one of the last issues of *The People* (No. 142) before he left England for the US in 1851: 'We are neither blind nor indifferent to their prejudice against colour: to their worship of gold; to their violent language; to their unseemly boasting; to their occasional excesses.' Those Chartists already resident in America would probably have added to this list: 'Self-culture is a good thing but it seemingly cannot abolish inequality nor restore men to their rights.'[2]

Consider the example of John C. Cluer from Glasgow, a former Chartist Temperance lecturer and associate of Devyr in the National Reform movement in New York. His field of operations in America encompassed most of the New England textile centres. In 1845 he scored a notable success on behalf of the working people of Lowell, and

---

[1] *Ibid.*, part II, p. 192.
[2] Orestes A. Brownson, *Boston Quarterly Review* (October, 1840). He was the editor of this radical magazine and a Christian Socialist. He was one of those who recognized the usefulness of T. A. Devyr to the cause, early in 1841.

over the course of the next few years became the best-known advocate for the Ten Hours movement in New England. And when war between Britain and America seemed to be the likely outcome of the Oregon controversy, he was instrumental in securing the passage of a resolution stating: 'Far from regarding the labouring man on the other side of the water as our enemy, and shooting him as such, we regard him as our friend and will do all in our power to better his condition.' He promptly followed this remarkable object lesson in workers' solidarity with a petition to the Massachusetts legislature asking for redress of the grievances of the textile operatives, and when the appeal went unheeded he tried his best to organize a 'general strike'. However, before he could put his 'master plan' into operation, the mill owners discovered that 'his respect for the institution of matrimony was less than profound' and turned his indiscretions against him. Cluer thereafter conducted his agitations in Boston where he was still a man of some stature among the working class leadership some 40 years later.[1]

Other Chartists whose reforming zeal was unimpaired by the failure of the movement in England, turned up in the chief coal mining regions of the US during the 'fifties and early 'sixties.[2] John Bates, for example, self-described as a man 'imbued with the lofty ideals of Chartism', founded in 1849 what was probably the first, even if short-lived, mine union in America.[3] Two other ex-Chartists, Daniel Weaver from Staffordshire and Thomas Lloyd from Wales, picked up the threads of mine unionism after Bates, undertaking organizational work in the coalfields of eastern Missouri and Southwest Illinois. Together in the early 'sixties, when the coal industry was in a state of war-boom, these two 'talked up the benefits to be derived from general organization'.[4] Weaver's insistence, in a pamphlet he published entitled *What Might be Done?*, that labour must learn how to exercise its power upon legislatures, was clearly a reflection of his Chartist background. Moreover, his plea: 'Let there be no English, no Irish, Germans, Scotch or Welsh! Rally round the standard of the Union—the union of the state and the unity of the miners,'[5] reflected not only his Chartist memory of time-wasting, divisive animosities, but also his unionist view of the Civil War then about to commence (though this was not a view shared by all ex-Chartists in America).

But, perhaps the most remarkable as well as the most successful of

---

[1] George McNeill, *The Labor Movement* (Boston, 1887), p. 105.
[2] Andrew Roy, *History of the Coal Miners of the US* (1907), p. 70.
[3] *Ibid.*, p. 75.   [4] McNeill, p. 244.   [5] *Ibid.*, p. 245.

the Chartist emigres who involved themselves in the American labour movement, was Thomas Ainge Devyr. His close collaboration with American labour leader, George Henry Evans, in a protracted struggle to win 'land for the landless', is the clearest example of Chartism reborn in the USA that it has been possible to find, and the fact that Feargus O'Connor took the keenest interest in it all along, suggests that he thought of it in this way also.[1]

The story of Devyr's years in America (1840–87) is a story of more than forty years of agitation for free farms, amongst other reforms, which did not end with President Lincoln's signature to the Homestead Act in 1862, but, because of Devyr's uncompromising nature, continued right up until his death in Brooklyn in 1887. It was first told by Devyr himself in his aptly titled, *The Odd Book*, which was published privately in 1882. It was not taken up by historians until Helene Zahler published her findings on the National Reform Association in 1941,[2] and then Professor Henry Christman combined these with his own research to produce a most absorbing narrative[3] subtitled, 'A Decisive Episode in the Emergence of Democracy'. This work revealed for the first time that Devyr's importance in the Free Soil movement was such that 'Devyrism', as his 'foreign' ideas for a new political party were called,[4] was a serious threat to the new 'Republican' group composed of dissident Whigs and Democrats, and had to be destroyed as a unified political force before that group could emerge as a new national party from the little Congregational Church of Ripon, Wisconsin, on 1 March 1854.

How that destruction was achieved, first by isolating the hot-headed and incautious Devyr from his more cautious followers, and then by separating the tenant farmers from the urban working-class radicals with whispered talk of 'agrarian socialism', is beyond the scope of this study. But Devyr's involvement with these Anti-Renters in the first place and as early as 1840, is most relevant here since this was a direct result of his initial disillusionment with American democracy, and reveals most strikingly his burning desire to recreate a Chartist situation —albeit an Irish one—on foreign soil.

Devyr, who had been a leading public figure in the Chartist movement in Newcastle upon Tyne and a secret 'commander' of a body of

---

[1] *Northern Star*, 20 and 27 April, 1 and 22 June, 6 and 20 July, 10 Aug., 14 Sept. 1844.
[2] Helene S. Zahler, *Eastern Workingmen and National Land Policy, 1829–62* (Columbia University Press, NY, 1941).
[3] Henry Christman, *Tin Horns and Calico* (New York, 1945).
[4] A term coined by Ira Harris, the man who finally discredited Devyr.

70 men, 'the most daring and desperate spirits in the movement' fully prepared 'to put Newcastle to the torch',[1] had to leave Newcastle in a hurry early in January 1840. He did so by walking with elaborate casualness and without any sort of baggage, across Tyne Bridge to Gateshead, with his friend and fellow Chartist, druggist John Rewcastle, shortly after they had been 'apprised that the local magistrates had got possession of all the particulars of our nightly muster. . . . The situation was just this. Assembling in arms, though not a blow struck, was an act of High Treason. No means to resist, and no thought of submission, I quitted the field.'[2] Pursued to Liverpool, they were almost arrested because they had unwisely given their real names at the shipping office. Luckily, their pursuers were delayed getting their warrants counter-signed by the Liverpool magistrates, and Devyr was able to persuade a boatman to take them out to the 'liner' *Independence*, which was moored in the Mersey. 'There was no steamer could catch her once she had set sail,' he was informed, and by the time his pursuers had returned to the docks they were on their way to America.[3] After a vain search of New York for employment, which lasted till the middle of April, he finally got a foothold. He was offered the editorship of the *Williamsburg Democrat* which was being launched to oppose the *Whig Star*,[4] and quickly became an accepted Democratic spokesman, ably exchanging volleys with Horace Greeley's campaign paper, *The Log Cabin*. By the end of 1840 he had become so useful to the party that it was suggested that he should go to Washington to continue his editorial work. At first he was elated, seeing a chance to make a comfortable living and wield great influence. But he had begun to suspect that the Democrats were not all that their name implied, and that the old abuses were not con-fined to England. 'Away with all ambition that has not for its object the welfare of the human race,' he wrote.[5] And, instead of going to Washing-ton, he turned the *Williamsburg Democrat* into a truly democratic paper. He began to agitate for railroads built and owned by the people, laws restricting wealth, freedom of the public land to actual settlers and limitations of land holding.

This stirred up the Hunker leaders and notification was sent to me that I must not publish such principles for the time to come. They were not

---

[1] *Odd Book, op. cit.*, pp. 200–207.
[2] *Ibid.*, p. 208. Both men had refused to take part in a 'mad' scheme, devised by Robert Peddie, to raid Alnwick Castle. See A. J. Peacock, *Bradford Chartism 1838–40* (York, 1969), pp. 40–45.
[3] *Ibid.*, pp. 209–11.
[4] *Odd Book*, American Section, p. 25.   [5] *Ibid.*, p. 33.

Plate 3

(a) Thomas Ainge Devyr

(b) W. J. Linton

(c) Matthew Mark Trumbull

(d) Andrew Carnegie

'Democratic' they said, 'because they were not adopted by the Party'. I suggested that they were essentially Democratic, and that the Party should adopt them or change its present name. At any rate they would get no 'monopolizing' Democracy from me. So they took away the Party advertising . . . and gave it to the *Whig Star*, there being only the two papers in the county. They also refused to pay me for what advertising I had done for them. And when I sued them they declared they would appeal it up, up to the highest court. I was unable to follow in such a flight, so I had to let it go.[1]

At this juncture, disillusioned and disheartened, Devyr happened to read a copy of the *Helderberg Advocate*, edited and published in Schoharie township, NY, by W. H. Gallup. Excited by Gallup's 'anathemas against the monster system' of patroonery,[2] he sent off letters to him at once encouraging resistance, citing Irish parallels and, above all, calling for freedom of the public land to settlers. As a result, after a series of such letters had been published in 1841 and early in 1842, he received an invitation to address a great Independence Day rally of tenant farmers at Rensslaerville in the Helderbergs in the summer of 1842. This, he recognized at once, was an opportunity he must seize with both hands, and he made sure, by visiting Albany ahead of time, that he had a thorough knowledge of the issues and the kind of people involved in the protest.[3]

His address to the farmers was a great success. Despite their reservations about his turning their cause into a national crusade, they were persuaded to sign a pact with Devyr: 'they to help me free the public lands to actual settlers only, I to aid them in their local war—write, attend their conventions—and made the condition that I should pay my own expenses'. As Professor Christman says: 'It was not the whole-hearted pledge of unity he wanted, and obviously he was promising more than they': but if he had to make some concessions to the conservatives in this instance, he and Dr. Smith A. Boughton[4] recovered lost ground when they helped draw up the Statement of Grievances and Proposed Redress. The radical imprint was plain upon it and it minced no words. Not only were the titles to the large estates illegal, but the

---

[1] *Ibid.*, p. 33.

[2] The establishment by the Dutch West India Company of patroonships or feudal manors, along the Hudson River, as a means of encouraging colonization, was continued by the English and extended to include 'deserving' English subjects. The unrest that followed these grants led to armed revolt in 1766. This was put down ruthlessly and the system even survived the Revolution in 1776, so great was the power of the landlords.

[3] *Odd Book*, p. 42.

[4] A local radical who had been involved in the 1837 Patriots' War in Canada.

leases that bound the tenants were unconstitutional since they contradicted the fundamental tenets of republican government. The tenants, directed by Devyr, asked for a constitutional amendment to end the leasehold system, pledged themselves to pay no rent until relief was secured, and committed themselves to a ten-year war if necessary.

Thus, for some considerable time before Devyr met up with George Henry Evans in New York in the spring of 1844—a meeting requested by Evans, newly emerged from semi-retirement, in order to launch a National Reform Party along the lines suggested by Devyr in his book, *Our Natural Rights*[1]—Devyr was himself the leader of an active movement for reform and had even begun the training of its members along the same para-military lines he had helped devise for his Chartists in Newcastle.[2] Like the Newcastle Chartists, they were bound by an oath secretly administered: unlike the Chartists, they went into action with remarkable success; and, though they brought the State troopers down on their heads, they provoked interesting political repercussions.

Even so, there is no doubt that it was George Evans who eventually took charge of the National Reformers. He was far more of a political realist as well as a more sober-headed leader. Quite clearly Devyr's 'guerilla' tactics helped to bring Silas Wright, the Governor of New York, to his knees in 1846 when, after years of stubborn defence of the rights of property, he suddenly found feudal tenures 'proper subjects' for legislative inquiry and discussion. But it was Evans who restrained Devyr from a reckless pursuit of the impossible, namely a unified political party, and, while he lived (he died in 1856) he remained leader and was content to see both National Reform and Anti-Rentism used merely as a wedge for the eventual reshuffling of the major parties.

Born in Herefordshire in 1804, of fairly well-to-do parents,[3] Evans was taken to the United States while still a child and apprenticed to a printer in Ithaca, NY, in 1820. Here he first read Thomas Paine and imbibed those principles which made him ever after, 'a firm and consistent infidel'.[4] Little more is known about his early years before he reached New York in 1829 and produced the first number of the *Working Man's Advocate* on 31 October 1829. But it was not long before his *Advocate* was the official organ of the city's first independent labour

---

[1] Republished with a Supplement on the United States, Williamsburg, New York, 1842.
[2] Christman, *op. cit.*, p. 74.
[3] His father was a commissioned officer.
[4] Lewis Masquerier, *Sociology or the Reconstruction of Society, Government and Property* (New York, 1877), p. 93.

party.[1] It was as the champion of free education, however, that Evans figured in the Working Men's Party and not as the exponent of free public land: in fact, the Working Men's Party paid small if any attention to this issue before being destroyed as an independent political force in 1831.[2] How then did Evans come to be concerned with the problem of land ownership?

Describing the evolution of his final career from 1844 to his death in 1856, Evans wrote that it was the proposals of Thomas Skidmore, a fellow printer who tried unsuccessfully to convert the Working Men's Party to his way of thinking in 1829, which first made him reflect on the general problem of land ownership.[3] But his conclusions, Evans claimed, were arrived at independently of Paine or Thomas Spence, and were fully shaped even before he had read Devyr's book, *Our Natural Rights*, which was first published in Belfast in 1836 and republished by Devyr in New York in 1842. What is certain is that it was during the years 1835–41, while quietly cultivating his 40-acre farm near Granville, New Jersey, that Evans developed his scheme of land reform based on the tenet of natural right. Prominent though he had been in the labour movement from 1829 to 1834, Evans fell somewhat into the background during the next two years. In August 1835 he moved to Rahway, New Jersey, where he continued to publish the *Advocate* until a serious illness and financial difficulties combined to keep him out of politics and out of print from February 1836 to January 1841.

Then 'very good friends to the cause' enabled him to speak out once more, even from his retirement. By June 1841, he was again presenting his ideas to the world in newspaper form, this time in *The Radical*. In September he was urged most strongly to return to New York and revive the *Working Man's Advocate* there, but he refused, saying that he was so disgusted with the accumulated miseries of cities that nothing but a desire to bring about a more rational state of affairs could ever induce him to reside in one again. By February 1844, however, he had forgotten his hatred of cities sufficiently to call a meeting in New York to hear the Irish Chartist, T. A. Devyr, describe his plan for political action in the area around Albany, NY.

By this time, Evans knew quite a bit about the activities of Devyr in Upper New York State through a mutual friend, Orestes Brownson of Boston. He was aware too of the stalemate situation in the Anti-Rent

[1] Zahler, *op. cit.*, p. 19.
[2] *Ibid.*, p. 22.
[3] *Working Man's Advocate*, second series, 16 Nov. 1844.

districts following the failure of the Anti-Rent petition to the New York legislature on 1 January 1844. But he was also aware that the farmers were now sufficiently aroused to want to implement Devyr's Chartist plan of direct action, namely para-military organization of the tenantry using the methods of the 'underground' movement.[1] Clearly this was a very good moment to revive the Working Men's Party and turn a local issue into a national crusade, and Evans did not hesitate. He quickly persuaded the other members of the meeting—which included former Chartist James T. Pyne, a picture-frame maker from Newcastle, as well as former members of the Working Men's Party and the Loco-Foco Party—to join forces with Devyr at once, using Devyr as the link between the revived labour movement in New York and the Anti-Renters in Upstate New York.

Soon after this meeting, the new group, calling itself the National Reform Association, issued a manifesto insisting that the only remedy for social injustice was a land policy that gave the worker an alternative to wage labour. Here was O'Connorism on American soil. Within a year, the conservative press was taking National Reform seriously enough to term it a 'menace';[2] but they had assumed, wrongly, that the success of the Anti-Rent movement was wholly the result of National Reform's 'pernicious preachments'. Actually, as Mike Walsh, one of the original members of the NRA insisted later, whatever attention National Reform attracted, it owed to the serious concern taken by wealthy New York landowners over the Anti-Rent leadership.[3] Evans, for his part, was most anxious to see the Anti-Rent tenants succeed and thus demonstrate to his urban workers that land reform was a better answer to their problems than 'pure and simple unionism'. With this in mind, therefore, he was forced to give over-much of the day-to-day leadership of the concerted struggle to Devyr, who overreached himself, presumed wrongly that he alone could unite the entire alliance, and thus allowed himself and his colleagues to be outmanœuvred by his opponents, led by Ira Harris.[4] Perhaps then, after all, there really was some truth as well as venom in Ira Harris's criticism of Devyr: 'Too vain and pre-sumptuous to act a subordinate part, he is too rash and indiscreet to be a leader.'[5] His vanity,[6] his assumption of infallible judgement,[7] his

[1] Christman, *op. cit.*, pp. 66–67.
[2] *United States Journal* (Washington, D.C.), 15 Nov. 1845.
[3] *Subterranean* (New York, N.Y.) *Weekly*, 24 April 1847.
[4] Christman *op. cit.*, pp. 266–67.   [5] Christman, p. 253.
[6] He believed firmly that he had started a movement that 'eventually led to the great Civil War'. (*Odd Book*, American Section, p. 41.)
[7] 'I communicated with Mr. Cowen (of Newcastle) very recently . . . If Mr.

ungovernable temper and unguarded tongue, together with his too frequent dictatorial manner,[1] most certainly marred his most promising early political career in America. On the other hand, he played a major part in helping to chart a new course for reform which eventually made free homes on the public domain a right of the actual settler instead of an act of charity to the poor. He did this by introducing Chartist methods of agitation as well as Chartist thinking into an unorganized, backward region of New York State, appealing to both farmer and workingman as only an Irishman of simple habits and simple courage could have done. He was defeated, partly by his own personal failings and his ignorance of the real nature of American democracy, but mainly by the superior tactics of the opposition who were able to distort his plan and win support for a sop instead of a genuine programme. But such is the fate of many reformers. If a reform measure seems to have popular appeal, it may be adopted for the sake of that appeal by those whose own interests are directly opposed. Thus it was with the National Reformers in their struggle to win 'land for the landless'.[2]

Devyr himself went on, after almost bankrupting himself on behalf of the Anti-Rent movement in 1846, to build up a small fortune by developing the East River waterfront in New York and accumulating four hundred building lots in Williamsburg. He spent most of this fortune endowing radical newspapers, with titles ranging from *The Taxpayers' Gazette* (1855) to *The Irish People* (1865–66), an organ of the Fenian Brotherhood, in the years between 1846 and 1874 when he was prompted to join the staff of *The Irish World*. This last 'bout of agitation' occurred as a result of 'the brutal press' coverage which the *New York Times* (21 March 1877) gave to the 'Judicial Murders' in the Pennsylvania coal mines,[3] and when Devyr was over 70 years of age.

Cowen takes up this work—this mission—all the Proletarians of England, in field and factory, will rally round his flag and make it a winding-sheet of land-thiefism.' (*Ibid.*, p. 219.)

[1] 1852 letter to Senator Shields of Illinois: 'If the Homestead Act now before the Senate be quietly passed into a law, it will produce a change in this world far greater than come over it when we made a new nation. Help that change if you be a man, if you be a Democrat . . . I will not go down on my knees . . . I will not kiss the dust at your feet and implore you to save this Republic from ruin.' (*Ibid.*, p. 82.)

[2] Coined by Devyr, this slogan was used by Republicans as late as 1888 (J. D. Long, *Repub. Party*, p. 111).

[3] 'Three Mollie Maguires were hanged at this place [Bloomsburg] today—Patrick Hester, Peter McHugh and Patrick Tully—all Irish Catholics, all middle-aged men, and all richly deserving of the halters that encircled their necks this morning. . . .' (*NYT*, 21 Mar. 1877.)

He had tried his best to raise a public outcry but had to admit to Patrick Ford, the editor of *The Irish World* that he would 'take no more trouble with a people that were so dull and apathetic'.[1] He was promptly invited to join the staff.

Mr. Ford introduced me with this very flattering notice:
It is with pleasure we announce that we have added to the staff of the *Irish World*, Mr. Thomas Ainge Devyr. His name is already known to the reader, and it is unnecessary to make any flourishes in this introduction. Mr. Devyr is a man of conscience and a man of ideas. He is a time-honored but by no means a time-worn reformer. His whole life has been devoted to the service of humanity; and now, moving toward three-score and ten, his one absorbing thought is to spend the remaining years that God shall give him in the same noble work.[2]

Devyr died in Brooklyn at the age of 82, on 27 May 1887.

[1] *Odd Book*, p. 173.
[2] *Ibid.*, p. 174. See also *Irish Times*, 31 March 1877.

6

Chartists and the slavery issue

The famous unanimity with which British workers condemned the Slave Power of the Confederacy and unwearingly sang the praises of Abolitionism, has been shown[1] to belong more to the mythology of Anglo-American relations during the Civil War than to the facts of history. Similarly, the idea that America was the nearest thing to perfection in this world except for the blemish of slavery, was not a belief shared unanimously by all British immigrants who had gone there during the Hungry Forties. They were, of course, all opposed to slavery, some more than others, but there were also many among them who were much more opposed to wage slavery than they were to negro slavery, and for them the war was largely irrelevant.

After its outbreak, it clearly became necessary for many ex-Chartists in America as well as for most Americans, to turn the war itself into something so strange, so different and mystical that it could only have happened to the chosen people. Moderate 'moral force' ex-Chartists, like M. M. Trumbull, readily agreed with John Bright that the war was being fought not over an American issue but a universal one.[2] 'There is nothing so worthy of reverence and obedience, and nothing more sacred, than the authority of the freely chosen by the majority of a great and free people.'[3] George Holyoake, another moderate as well as a travelling journalist who kept in close touch with his ex-comrades, was also speaking for many ex-Chartists when he wrote in 1865 that, 'If the South could set up a Slave Empire, the working class of England would

[1] Most recently by R. Harrison in his *Before the Socialists* (London, 1965), pp. 40 ff.
[2] See dedication to M. M. Trumbull's *The Free Trade Struggle in England* (Chicago, 1882).
[3] Bright to Sumner, 6 Sept. 1861. Quoted by Lillibridge, *op. cit.*, p. 120.

be told to be thankful that they are allowed the liberty they have instead of seeking for more.'[1]

But there was a far more emotional and a much more peculiar view of the Civil War prevalent among the more economically oppressed British immigrants in the overcrowded eastern cities, as well as among the more class-conscious ex-Chartist lieutenants in America, such as J. F. Bray, T. A. Devyr and John Campbell. For them, the popular mythology that America was unique and fundamentally different from all previous nations, had been seriously undermined long before the Civil War. They, and particularly Devyr and Campbell, had stubbornly offset this disillusionment with a clear and unequivocal preference for American government over British government. But none of them, not even Campbell who was almost a 'Copperhead' at one stage of the war, let their new patriotism overshadow their much deeper and long-standing opposition to the industrial revolution, which had followed them so relentlessly across the Atlantic.

Little is known about John Campbell (1810–74), the Irish-born Lancashire weaver, prior to his emergence on the Chartist scene in Manchester in 1840 and his election to the paid executive as Secretary to the National Charter Association in 1841.[2] Just 31 years of age when appointed secretary,[3] he was one of a group of Irish Chartists in Manchester (they included James Leach, Christopher Doyle, John Linney and John Deegan[4]) who shared an ideology and a concept of social justice centred on the land rather than the towns.[5] He was also responsible for an undated pamphlet, entitled *An Examination of the Corn and Provision Laws from their First Enactment to the Present Period*, as well as the oft-quoted remark made during the Plug Plot strikes in Manchester: 'Not a single mill at work! Something must come out of this, and something serious!'[6]

His American career (1843–74) is, however, of some historic importance if only because he wrote and published several books there, at his own expense, which reveal a rather surprising and very special Chartist emigre attitude towards negro slavery in America. It is a view-

---

[1] G. J. Holyoake, *The Liberal Situation* (London, 1865), p. 48.

[2] *Northern Star*, 7 June 1841.

[3] He is dismissed by Hovell, p. 199, as 'a man of no great ability or importance'.

[4] Deegan, the representative for Hyde and Glossop, fled to the US in the spring of 1841 after he had been 'tried' by his peers at Sunderland for speaking against the *Northern Star*'s editorial policy.

[5] See Rachel O'Higgins' *Ireland and Chartism* (Dublin, 1959), pp. 3–4.

[6] *Life of Thomas Cooper*, p. 206.

point diametrically opposed to that held by most British workers at the time and shared only by a very few ex-Chartists such as W. J. Dunning,[1] who did not emigrate, as well as by those such as John Francis Bray and Thomas Ainge Devyr, who did. It can be summarized as an extremely conservative and pro-slavery viewpoint, inexplicable at first, even though a closer examination of it reveals that, at bottom, it was not really concerned with negro slavery at all but rather with what they considered to be the far greater iniquities of wage slavery, which most Abolitionists preferred to ignore.

It is significant that Campbell dedicated his very first piece of polemical writing[2] to 'the agricultural serfs and factory slaves of Great Britain and Ireland'. He appealed to them as 'fellow labourers. I am one of yourselves, a hard-working man, a Fustian Jacket, as [Feargus] O'Connor terms us.' If, he continues, the working classes could see that the interest of the workingman is the same in every country, the power of the oppressor would soon be destroyed. 'The industrious classes are never thought of (by the landlords and the lords of the long chimneys) except to be worked like horses, and fed like asses, both on the land and in the mills, in order that gold may be coined out of their sweat and blood, for their merciless task-masters.'[3]

Despite a growing reputation based on such violent, class-conscious language, Campbell did and said nothing when asked to give them his guidance by the leaders of the Plug Plot strikes. However, on 20 September 1842, he was arrested nevertheless, and charged with 'sedition, conspiracy, tumult and riot' in the famous trial 'Feargus O'Connor, Esq. and fifty-eight others', at Lancaster, March 1843. Released on a technicality, he decided to emigrate at once in case he should be re-arrested. Perhaps he also wished to avoid certain of his fellow Chartists who claimed they had discovered minor but sizeable discrepancies in his official book-keeping while he was in prison.[4] Later that same year, he appeared in Philadelphia[5] where he embarked on a long career as a bookseller and small publisher after an initial period as a weaver.[6] In

---

[1] See R. Harrison, *Before the Socialists* (London, 1965), pp. 43–45.
[2] Published by Abel Heywood (Manchester, 1841 ?), and mentioned above, p. 58.
[3] Quoted by Jos. Dorfman, *The Economic Mind in American Civilization*, vol 2 (New York, 1946), p. 690.
[4] *NS*, 7 Jan. 1843.
[5] English and Northern Irish handloom weavers, attracted by wages three and four times those at home, firmly established the fine cotton-goods trade of Philadelphia. See M. T. Copeland, *The Cotton Mfg. Industry of the US* (Cambridge, 1912), p. 31.
[6] He had been living in the same house in Oldham St., Manchester, as his

1844 he was the first secretary of the Social Reform Society, then came others with such names as the Social Improvement Society. At the same time, he tried to control the Philadelphia labour movements. He also became Horace Greeley's Philadelphia correspondent in labour matters and received letters from various ex-Chartists as a result of his articles in the *New York Tribune*.[1] Clearly he thought himself a power in his new land because he did not hesitate to appeal to the outstanding Democratic leader in the state, James Buchanan, for a loan of $327. He specified as a condition 'that you will give me my own time to pay you'. Naturally, he reminded Buchanan, 'my influence with the working class is great', and concluded with the admonition, 'I never forsook a friend or forgot a friend.'[2] But he was turned down.

In 1848 he published a small book of 127 pages, dedicated to Louis Blanc for his brave efforts in leading 'the proletarians' against 'the bourgeoisie', entitled *A Theory of Equality; or the Way to Make Every Man Act Honestly*. More of a recruiting pamphlet for the Democratic Party (of which he was a member) than a reformist tract, it contains a strong argument for land reform and suggests he was aware of Devyr's activities in Albany, NY,[3] if only through Greeley. Aware here that his proposals were not new, he informed the public through the *New York Tribune* (22 May 1850) that: 'I obtained them twenty years ago from James Bronterre O'Brien, who obtained them from the French school of 1793.' He also mentions his indebtedness to John Francis Bray, then resident in Pontiac, Michigan,[4] from whose *Labour's Wrongs* he borrowed twenty consecutive pages as 'illustrative material'.

But, turning to his views on slavery as expressed in his *Negro-Mania: being an Examination of the Falsely Assumed Equality of the Various Races of Men* (Philadelphia, Campbell and Power, 1851),[5] it is not difficult to see why a close friend and associate could say of him at this time: 'he acted first and thought afterwards . . . and soon became

---

Treasurer and publisher friend, Abel Heywood (in order to keep the Chartist records under close supervision) and doubtless learnt a lot about the publishing business from him.

[1] Dorfman, *op. cit.*, p. 691.
[2] *Ibid.*, p. 693.
[3] See below, p. 66.
[4] See below, p. 69.
[5] In fairness, he openly states on p. 3, 'I do not profess any originality, but I lay claim to some tact in the arrangement of my quotations . . . when I know that it would take hundreds of dollars to purchase all the books that I have read upon the subject, and when I also know that but few poor men have the means of obtaining these books, I therefore have attempted to popularize this question by citing such portions of the best authors as have written upon it.'

a marked man among the most violent of extremists'.[1] His book, 'a violent and one-sided diatribe', did not meet with public favour 'and was the cause of financial embarrassment'.[2] It is indeed a long book and must have been expensive to produce: it comprises some 549 pages, most of which are taken up with extracts from other works. Only near the end (pp. 469–70) does he reveal anything like a rational attitude towards slavery and, at the same time, his prime motive for writing the book:

I know it may be said that these remarks are trivial and perhaps ill-natured, but it is absolutely necessary that citizens at a distance should know and appreciate that philanthropy which will encourage the negro to rob his master, but which will not lift a finger in behalf of the oppressed and degraded of their own race. Nor do I believe that the New York or New England abolitionists have ever accomplished or attempted to accomplish anything for their white brethren. Pennsylvania has a ten hour law, New Jersey has another, but no thanks to the abolitionists. The fact is, that some of the bitterest opponents of the ten hour system are rank, rabid abolitionists.

Campbell then goes on to quote admiringly as well as extensively[3] from a famous speech by 'one of the most rabid champions of negro slavery in the US Senate',[4] James H. Hammond from South Carolina, and in so doing illustrates the real success that his and other disruptive Southern propaganda was having at this time, particularly among those alien workmen (most of whom were English) in the forefront of the rapidly growing labour movement in the Northern States. Here is a typical example of Hammond's persuasive language, addressed, it will be noted, primarily to Englishmen:

If a man steals a pig in England, he is transported—torn from wife, children, parents, and sent to the Antipodes, infamous, and an outcast forever, though perhaps he took from the superabundance of his neighbour to save the lives of his famishing little ones. If one of our well fed negroes, merely for the sake of fresh meat, steals a pig, he gets perhaps forty stripes. If one of your cottagers breaks into another's house, he is hung for burglary. If a slave does the same here, a few lashes, or perhaps a few hours in the stocks, settles the matter. Are our courts or yours the most humane?[5]

Surprisingly, Campbell does not include the following opening

---

[1] W. Brotherhead, *Forty Years Among the Old Booksellers of Philadelphia* (Philadelphia, 1891), pp. 38–39.
[2] *Ibid.*, p. 39.
[3] He fills sixteen pages with only a portion of the full speech.
[4] H. Schluter, *Lincoln, Labor and Slavery* (NY, 1913), p. 114.
[5] Quoted by Campbell in *Negro-Mania*, pp. 482–83.

sentences from Hammond's speech but he was surely greatly affected by them:

> The Senator from New York said yesterday that the whole world had abolished slavery. Aye, the name, but not the thing; all the powers of the earth cannot abolish it. God only can do it when he repeals the fiat, 'the poor ye always have with you'; for the man who lives by daily labor, and scarcely lives at that, and who has put out his labor in the market and take the best he can for it—in short, your whole hireling class of manual laborers and 'operatives', as you call them, are essentially slaves. The difference between us is, that our slaves are hired for life and well compensated. . . .[1]

It is easy now perhaps to convict the South Carolina senator of mis-representing the social conditions of the South. But it must have been difficult indeed, if not impossible, for newly arrived aliens in the 1850's. It was also very difficult to refute his statements concerning Northern capitalist development and its likely consequences for free workingmen. The coming conflict between the North and the South was clearly not the only 'irrepressible conflict': there was also the impending conflict between free workingmen and industrial capitalists which Hammond could see almost as plainly as could ex-Chartists like Campbell, Devyr and Bray.

Devyr, for example, summed up his views and those of many of his fellow Chartists when he wrote in the *New York Tribune*, 16 February 1850: 'Emancipate the white man first: free him from the thraldom of his unsupplied wants and the day this is done, we'll commence the manumission of the much wronged black man within our borders.' John Francis Bray's views on slavery were in general accord with this statement, at least until the middle of the war itself, when he was moved to make his most misunderstood remark: 'The world is full of wrongs: but African slavery . . . is not one of the most heinous that afflicts either the black or the white race.'[2] Now this 'surprising statement' from such a gentle, studious soul, living on a lonely farm in Michigan and very much 'hors du combat', is easy enough to understand when read in context. Clearly he meant no more than a show of impatience. For him the cries against African slavery were simply irrelevant to the main evil of capitalism, which had to be reformed before mankind could live happily with itself.

In other words, he was not deranged: he was not up to 'strange in-

---

[1] Schluter, *op. cit.*, p. 114.
[2] *American Destiny* (NY, 1864), p. 14.

consistent antics', as Dorfman assumes[1]—unless his recognition of 'old Wilberforce' in all that he saw of hypocrisy in the abolitionist ranks, was derangement. Perhaps it was: it is dangerous to speculate on such matters. On the other hand, what interest had English workmen in a struggle for mastery in America between slave-owners and enterprising capitalists, who wanted foreign labour 'mainly to break strikes and who worshipped nothing but the almighty dollar'?[2] Unlike certain other veterans of Chartism, such as Harney, Ernest Jones, Lloyd Jones and M. M. Trumbull, these three most militant and class-conscious ex-Chartists were totally unwilling to acknowledge that wage labour was an advance upon slavery. They conceived of exploitation as an abstraction, an 'essence' whose changes of form were utterly irrelevant. They simply and passionately hated white slavery and this hatred came very near to turning into a defence of negro slavery through their fear and jealousy.[3] Moreover, their obvious confusion at being at variance with the old Chartist tradition of sympathy for the North American Republic and of opposition to slavery, helps to throw some light on the predicament of those who expressed confederate sympathies in England among the working classes.

Chartists like M. M. Trumbull, on the other hand, regarded this exploitation in a more historical light and therefore more optimistically. 'Not for ever shall the greed of privileged classes rob the laborer of the profits of his toil. Every day the workingmen are learning something new. By and by they will know their duty and organize their power. Then the moral force of a great cause, backed by a voting strength invincible, will put them in possession of their great estate.'[4] Ernest Jones was another Chartist veteran who was among the most passionate and active supporters of the Federal cause.[5] George Julian Harney resigned his editorship of the *Jersey Independent* rather than submit to the wishes of the proprietors who sympathized with the Confederacy.[6] Lloyd Jones, who worked for the *Glasgow Sentinel*, also preferred to

[1] Dorfman, *op. cit.*, p. 962.
[2] See *Bee-Hive*, 26 March 1864 (article by George Troup).
[3] Since Devyr and Campbell were both Catholics, it is of some importance here that most Catholic papers in Eastern cities were anti-Abolition. After emancipation, they argued, the negro worker would crowd out the white worker, particularly the Irish. And, since the Catholic church did nothing to counteract this newspaper argument, it too acquired the reputation of being 'a protagonist of slavery'. (P. S. Foner, *Hist. of Labor Movt. in the US*, (NY, 1947), pp. 269–70.)
[4] *Wheelbarrow*, *op. cit.*, pp. 161–62.
[5] J. Saville, *Ernest Jones: Chartist* (London, 1952) pp. 77 f.
[6] *Jersey Independent*, 29 Nov. 1862.

resign rather than lend his pen to the Slave Power.[1] All of these, it seems, found no difficulty in acknowledging that wage labour was a real advance upon slavery. They obviously had no desire to undo the work of the industrial revolution, like some of their sourer, old compatriots. Instead, they saw things as they were at the time and how they could well be in the future (assuming, of course, the moral improvement of mankind) with a statesmanlike sense of the historical development of the 'destiny' of labour, which was remarkably optimistic considering the 'sauve qui peut' American context in which most Chartist emigres found themselves.

[1] J. M. Ludlow, 'Some of the Christian Socialists of 1848 and the Following Years', *Economic Review*, Jan. 1894.

7

The Americanization of Chartism

Those ex-Chartists on both sides of the Atlantic who remained unreconciled to capitalism despite the evidence of the unprecedented industrial expansion during the 1850's, proceeded to air their criticisms of American democracy with remarkable frankness after the outbreak of the American Civil War. Those in England did so largely because America had been the repository of all their hopes for social democracy —and had destroyed them. Those in America still (many having returned to Britain during the previous decade),[1] felt this way also but with certain important reservations. All were critical, however, and thereby revealed not merely their basic misunderstanding of American democracy but also how much further than their old compatriots they had travelled since their Chartist days. Then, many of them might well have been satisfied with some redistribution of property and political power in terms of male equality. Now, most of them would clearly not rest until they had seen at least the dawning of an era when fundamental social change would produce a community of propertied equals.

During the early stages of the war, the hostile attitude of the English labour press towards the Federal side was so shrill and intemperate that it cannot be adequately explained simply by referring to the reported confusion and ambiguity of Federal war aims. Nor is it sufficient to add to this such contributory factors as the diplomatic blunders of Seward, the news of the appalling death roll at Bull Run, and the obvious dependence of working-class papers for news about America on middle-class news sources.[2] There was clearly a much more compelling motive

---

[1] Official figures indicate that 18,814 immigrants returned from North America to the UK in 1858. The momentum continued throughout 1860, when 17,798 persons from the US and 1,098 from British North America recrossed the Atlantic. (See W. S. Shepperson, *Emigration and Disenchantment*, University of Oklahoma, 1965, p. 25.)

[2] See Royden Harrison, *op. cit.*, chapter II.

behind this hostility than the simple business of selling newspapers, and the probability that it was largely a reflection of frustration and anger over the 'perversion' of American democracy, is increased to near certainty when we further examine the strange and ambiguous attitudes to the war taken up by ex-Chartists in America such as J. F. Bray and John Campbell.

Campbell, for instance, had, like most Chartists, revealed his almost proprietorial attitude towards American democracy in his *A Theory of Equality*, published in 1848, which was only a very short time after his arrival:

Andrew Jackson was a worthy successor of Jefferson. . . . But has the party itself been true to its principles? Has the party been consistent advocates and defenders of the rights of man? Has it, where it has had the power, destroyed paper money in each state? Has it made the land of the United States free to actual settlers? Has it established free trade? Has it abrogated usury? Has it abolished slavery? Has it prevented monopoly? I ask for proofs. If it has not done these things, and I contend it has not, then it should no longer be styled the Democracy.[1]

Later, during the Civil War, in his book *Unionists versus Traitors*, Campbell, like Bray, suddenly discovered a most personal, 'foreign' and novel cause for 'our present difficulties'. It is almost an outsider's view of the Civil War:

In reviewing the causes of our present difficulties, let me state one of the most prolific sources. It is Official Corruption. On every hand we witness this general depravity. Conventions are bought and sold: nominations are sought by the most vicious men. . . . This course is not confined to one party—it pervades all.[2]

This sort of eccentricity, together with his peculiar views on slavery, suggests that Campbell had now become more than a little over-wrought by what he repeatedly termed 'these perversions of democracy'.[3] Originally one of a group of Irish Chartists in Manchester who shared an ideology and a concept of social justice centred on the land rather than the towns,[4] Campbell had been as optimistic as T. A. Devyr over the National Reform struggle to win 'land for the landless'. This, he said in an open letter to Horace Greeley, 'will save this Republic from

[1] *A Theory of Equality; or The Way to Make Every Man Act Honestly* (Philadelphia, 1848), chapter IV, p. 20.
[2] *Unionists versus Traitors* (Philadelphia, 1861), p. 7.
[3] *Ibid.*, p. 8.
[4] See Rachel O'Higgins, 'The Irish Influence on the Chartist Movement', *Past and Present*, vol. xx (November 1961), pp. 84–85.

ruin. If you be a Democrat, help that change.'[1] Unfortunately, while Greeley accepted Campbell's contention that nothing but free public land could remedy workers' grievances, the Democratic Party as a whole was opposed to the Homestead Bill which was denied the people until 1862 when the Republican Party made a version of it law. Campbell, unlike Devyr, could not bring himself to resign from the party. He was a prominent member of the Douglas wing of the party in Philadelphia, and lived in hopes of changing some of the party policies.[2] But there is no doubt of his mental turmoil at this time. He complains, for example, that, 'although they are often unemployed, Americans boast of their economic advantages; although they condemn politicians, they defend a corrupt political system'.[3] He would probably also have added, as Bray did a little later in the war, that although they advocate freedom, Americans go to war to enforce conformity. 'The freedom of slaves and the slavery of states is a republican contradiction. An existing status may make slaves of each, but the right of secession sets both free.'[4]

Small wonder then that Campbell, irritated beyond endurance by 'these perversions of democracy', suddenly threw open his bookshop to any and every enemy of the government of the day, and openly defied the law, just as his guide and mentor, Abel Heywood of Manchester, had done in his Chartist days.

His store became the centre for hot-headed Democrats who opposed the government in its action. Many arrests were made, and a number of them were imprisoned. Then came the issue of habeas corpus. Pamphlets were issued by the dozen in favour of habeas corpus. John Campbell's store was the hotbed of this clique of men. Pamphlets were issued from this centre and it became widely known through the country and gained the sympathy and encouragement of the Copperheads generally. Campbell had the courage of his opinions, and violently advocated his right for the benefit of his acts. It may be said that this action was in entire harmony with his previous political career in England.[5]

John Francis Bray, on the other hand, who became almost as eccentric in his views on the war as Campbell, was never in any doubt about his attitude towards American democracy. For him, it was the same in 1864 as it had been in 1842 when he left England to return as an adult to his

---

[1] *New York Tribune*, 16 July 1852.

[2] Dorfman, *op. cit.*, pp. 689–93 (vol. 2).

[3] Campbell, *Unionists*, *op. cit.*, p. 9.

[4] J. F. Bray, *American Destiny: What shall it be, Republican or Cossack?* (New York, 1864), p. II.

[5] William Brotherhead, *Forty Years among the Old Booksellers of Philadelphia* (Philadelphia, 1891), pp. 36–41.

homeland. 'The vulture-monger is the same, whether he be called a monarchist or a republican',[1] is how he expressed himself in 1839. And this was his considered opinion in the middle of the war, some twenty-five years later: 'The question of free labour is one to be decided in the future, for the present has not yet comprehended it . . . If a man drives a starvation bargain with poor sewing girls, his case is precisely that of the slave holder.'[2]

Alone among his Chartist compatriots in having some knowledge of American democracy in advance of his emigration, Bray believed very strongly that American democracy had long since been totally perverted: 'If the free institutions of the Americans were acted up to, no slavery, whether of black men or white, could exist in that country. But the spirit of equality, on which these institutions are founded, is unfelt and unknown by the people—and why is it so? Because there are two classes—a class to labour, and a class to control labour—the first poor and the last rich.'[3] Bray was also unafraid of being called unpatriotic. Among Bray's manuscripts is a hand-written page that says: 'Sent to *The Hartford Examiner*, Feb. 10.' It has no other identification. It reads: 'One of the greatest frauds of our day is "loyalty to the government". It came up with us during the war and has been bawled ever since by the politicians that constitute the "government". It means, not loyalty to your own convictions, not loyalty to truth and justice, not loyalty to the republic and/or its principles, but slavish obedience to any political organ that may be enthroned in Washington.'[4] Clearly, he found little cause to change his views during his long years in America from 1842 to his death in 1897, except to get a little impatient from time to time. In his first and best known book, *Labour's Wrongs*, for example, he carefully avoids any kind of compulsion, which would in any case be a very bad foundation on which to build a system of co-operation between capital and labour. It was much later in his life that Bray, apparently becoming impatient with the slow progress of the new social order, half-heartedly advocated 'compulsory co-operation'. Writing in the *Detroit Socialist*, he stated: 'It is not sufficient to contend for shorter hours and more pay. This does not cover half the ground. It does not touch the issue of the serfdom of labor to capital. . . . At the basis must lie a declaration of the independence of labour from the

---

[1] J. F. Bray, *Labour's Wrongs, op. cit.*, p. 19.
[2] J. F. Bray, *American Destiny, op. cit.*, pp. 13, 16.
[3] J. F. Bray, *Labour's Wrongs, op. cit.*, p. 20.
[4] In the John Francis Bray Papers, Labadie Collection, University of Michigan General Library, Ann Arbor, Michigan.

control of capital, with its rights to self-government and self-employ-
ment. Things will have to be forced to an issue, there is no other way.'[1]

This, of course, was an interesting lapse for a 'missionary' like Bray
to make and should be seen as an example of that split-mindedness, or
dualism, present in and troubling to many early socialists. As Bray says
of himself in his 'Brief Sketch': 'He believed in co-operation and
community living but he was also an individualist and liked to be his
own boss.' Like most emigrants, he had tried farming when he became
unemployed for the first time in Boston. Finding the job-market in
Boston in a depressed state similar to that which he had just left in
England, he struck out for the west—and was momentarily tempted by
the vision of himself as a property-holder. He had never farmed. He
had never even cut down a tree. Perhaps his Owenite ideology led him
to think of farming initially. Certainly he, like many British immigrants
at this time, was a civilized man sick of civilization and in search of new
purpose and direction. But he soon found himself enjoying more than
the simple pleasures of natural independence. Describing his initial
success in Lapeer, Michigan, in a letter to his aunt in Leeds, Yorks.,
Mrs. Anne Bray Gawler, Bray enthused: 'I now have over 80 acres of
land, this barn which is now finished and about 15 pounds in money.
So you see I am getting along very well and do not owe a penny. I am
much better off than I should ever have been in England and have no
fear of want of employment.'[2] Here was the man of property speaking
rather than just a simple farmer, and perhaps he was disturbed by this
dualism because he suddenly sold the farm and moved to Pontiac,
Michigan, in 1848. There he returned to his old trade as editor–printer
of the *Pontiac Jacksonian*. He was never tempted again. Indeed, the
wonder is that he ever became a farmer at all, since he was a very little
man, only five feet four inches in height and weighing barely 100
pounds.[3] His true *métier* was polemical writing and this he knew by the
time he had made himself ill trying to be a farmer and a printer in
Detroit, at one and the same time, in order to pay off his farm loan.
Typical of his mature view of a socialist future on both sides of the
Atlantic, is the following:

The agriculturalists of Ireland and England must have access to the
stolen estates of the nobility, and the wage workers of all nations must
claim the use of all the mines, manufactures and machinery which their

[1] *Detroit Socialist*, 12 Jan. 1878.
[2] Letter dated 1 Feb. 1847. Labadie Collection, Ann Arbor, Michigan.
[3] J. F. Bray's passport details. *Ibid.*

labours have called into existence. There is no other remedy for our social evils.[1]

But this was a viewpoint which Bray had held steadily most of his life, unlike certain 'conservative' Chartists such as M. M. Trumbull, James Charlton and W. J. Linton, who only arrived at such an extreme solution towards the end of their lives in America—and then, only after an almost traumatic shock. They had never subscribed to the socialist view of what a true democracy should be—until the Anarchist hangings of 11 November 1886. Then and only then did they emerge from their American retreats and dare to reveal themselves as social democrats in all but name.

When General Matthew Mark Trumbull, a well-known but only moderately successful Chicago lawyer and writer, died at his home in Chicago on 10 May 1894, the following obituary notice appeared in *The Athenaeum*:

The death is announced of Gen. M. M. Trumbull at Chicago on the 11th ult. aged 68. General Trumbull, who was a native of London, emigrated to America 47 years ago, served with distinction in the Civil War and held various offices in that country. His chief works are, 'The Free Trade Struggle in England' and 'Articles & Discussions on the Labour Question'. He was connected with The Monist and The Open Court in Chicago, and had long been a voluminous contributor to American periodicals on economic and philosophical subjects.[2]

Thus was a former radical's adventurous life trimmed and groomed to fit him for inclusion with the respectable dead who had contributed to the sober pages of this worthy English magazine. No mention here of his youthfully expressed desire to overthrow the British monarchy;[3] nor of his early life as a tramping bricklayer's labourer over the length and breadth of England. No mention, in fact, of anything to allow the entry to compete for interest with the real life of M. M. Trumbull, an ex-Chartist who, like Andrew Carnegie, rose from rags to riches in a way that gave almost unbelievable reality to the Horatio Alger myth. But then Trumbull had spent most of his adult life consciously resisting being turned into a proletarian. In the brief autobiographical sketch which prefaces his *Articles on the Labor Question*, he refers most feelingly to 'a youth spent in poverty and a life that might have amounted to something' had it not been for his father's imprisonment for debt[4] when

---

[1] Excerpt from article, 'The Seeds of Revolution', signed J.F.B. which appeared in the *Detroit Advance and Labour Leaf*, 10 Sept. 1887.

[2] *The Athenaeum*, 2 June 1894, no. 3475, p. 713.

[3] *Wheelbarrow*, *op. cit.*, pp. 16–41, 249.

[4] Imprisonment for debt was not abolished in England until 1869.

Trumbull was only three years old. From that moment, it is made clear that for Trumbull (as for Charles Dickens) the descent from the possibility of some sort of middle-class education (his father, like Dickens senior, having owned a shop) to manual labour, was a descent into the nethermost hell, the denial to him of everything that made life worthwhile, an injury never to be forgotten and never to be forgiven.

My parents being poor, it was natural that I should as early as possible help them to earn our living. At thirteen I was lucky enough to get a job of work at a dollar and a quarter a week and 13 hours a day. . . . I need not say how hard, premature and grinding the labor was: the memory of it is too bitter; so let it pass. At the time I speak of the lines of caste were sharply drawn in England and I was duly instructed to 'Fear God, Honor the King, and be contented in that station of life which it had pleased God to give me' . . . When the facts of our lives are considered it will not be surprising that we ceased to honor the King or to fear God. We became Chartists . . . ready to storm the Tower of London as the Frenchmen stormed the Bastille. I made imitation Jacobin speeches as bombastic as the real ones, and I wrote 'red' poetry for the Northern Star, the fiery organ of the Chartist party.[1]

Having consciously hated the students at Cambridge while working as a building labourer among the colleges there prior to his emigration,[2] he explains that he chose the US Army and the law as professions because they 'obliterated his past', by which he meant his working-class origins. They also clearly helped the Americanization process because, by the spring of 1857, he had not only fought in Mexico with the army, but had also passed his Bar exams and been elected to the Iowa legislature. He was now, he says smugly, 'an American statesman and I played the part with perfect satisfaction to myself'.[3] His general outlook at this time is summed up as follows: 'Individual ambition and an active personal conscience are the levers by which the working men must lift themselves. Self-reform is the true tonic for exhausted labour. . . A maudlin trust in "government" will accomplish nothing.'[4] Now this would seem to be Trumbull's version not so much of Samuel Smiles and 'Self-Help', which it resembles, as of the Jeffersonian ideals of intense individualism combined with duty, which, he says in his autobiography, he began to study seriously while serving in the army for the second time.[5] But, while this sort of Americanizing study may have

---

[1] *Wheelbarrow, op. cit.*, pp. 17–20.
[2] *Ibid.*, p. 156.
[3] *Ibid.*, pp. 36–37.
[4] *Ibid.*, pp. 204–205.
[5] M. M. Trumbull, *Thomas Jefferson—Father of American Democracy* (Chicago, 1880).

Attention Workingmen!

GREAT

MASS MEETING

TO-NIGHT, at 7.30 o'clock,

AT THE

HAYMARKET, Randolph St., Bet. Desplaines and Halsted.

Good Speakers will be present to denounce the latest atrocious act of the police, the shooting of our fellow-workmen yesterday afternoon.

THE EXECUTIVE COMMITTEE.

Achtung Arbeiter!

Große

Maſſen-Verſammlung

Heute Abend, halb 8 Uhr, auf dem

Heumarkt, Randolph-Straße, zwiſchen Desplaines- u. Halſted-Str.

☞ Gute Redner werden den neueſten Schurkenſtreich der Polizei, indem ſie geſtern Nachmittag unſere Brüder erſchoß, geißeln.

Das Executiv-Comite.

Fig. 4. Facsimile of a handbill, Chicago 1886

opened Trumbull's eyes to the fact that the Jefferson–Lincoln ideal was out-of-date in industrial America, and that a small part of the ideal, the material success part, had come to do duty for the whole—it does not explain how this rather self-satisfied, 'compassionate conservative', ex-Chartist 'moderate', became a most deeply concerned, publicly active, social democrat in the years when he was resident in Chicago, from 1882 to his death in 1894.

It was not until the dramatic events of May 1886 that Trumbull emerged from obscurity onto the political scene as an outraged lawyer demanding clemency for the wrongfully convicted anarchists, Parsons, Spies, Fischer, Eugel, Fielden, Schwab, Neebe and Lingg.[1] But as his protests became more widely publicized and investigated by the hostile press, it was revealed that he had shared a public platform with several of the anarchists in the months preceding their arrest, and that his interest in them was deeper than the legal process involved. It seemed he had not only engaged in 'many public and private controversies with the anarchists, Spies and Parsons'; but was a friend of 'the Englishman Fielden'. He was, naturally enough, a strong opponent of their theory of reform by violence and, in public debate with them, 'declared roundly that no change for the better is possible except through moral forces'.[2] On the other hand, he also believed firmly that judges who violate the law, especially in their official capacity, are more guilty than delinquents of inferior degree, and that the law was being strangled in the Chicago courts in order that the accused anarchists might be strangled on the gallows.

On 3 November 1886, he urged Mrs. Lucy Parsons, the Mexican wife of anarchist Albert Parsons, to sell as many copies as she could of his 70-page pamphlet, *Was it a Fair Trial?* and keep the proceeds for her husband's defence. She managed to sell 5,000 copies on a Chicago street-corner—but it was no use. The four men, Parsons, Spies, Fischer and Eugel, were hanged on 11 November without appeal, which immediately convinced the shocked Trumbull that he must now give all his attention to his polemical writings. 'With the most radical temper he could summon up at his ripening age',[3] (he was now aged 60), he entered into a close association with Dr. Paul Carus, the Positivist editor of *The Open Court* magazine, one of the principal radical thinkers' magazines of the day, and eagerly accepted the posts of assistant editor

---

[1] Henry David, *The History of the Haymarket Affair* (New York, 1936), pp. 440–41.
[2] M. M. Trumbull, *The Trial of the Judgement* (Chicago, 1888), p. 75.
[3] Dr. Paul Carus in *The Open Court*, vol. VIII (1894), p. 4080.

and regular columnist. His old association with Thomas J. Morgan and George Schilling, both prominent socialists, ripened to the point where 'he was publicly branded as a demagogue and a sower of discontent';[1] but his friendship with Henry Demarest Lloyd, a leading middle-class radical, enabled him to get the widest possible support for his Amnesty Association which was ultimately successful in securing pardons for the three remaining anarchists, among whom was the former Lancashire cotton operative and son of a Chartist, Samuel Fielden of Todmorden.

Fig. 5.   Samuel Fielden (1847–1921)

Fielden, variously described as an anarchist, a professional agitator, a socialist and a former Methodist revivalist, seems to have been a remarkable personality. One newspaper correspondent, giving his age as 40, stated, 'He is broad-shouldered and strong, has red cheeks, a bushy beard, a low forehead and eyes deep-set. He is a painter by trade, but is really a professional agitator.' According to an extract from a Chicago newspaper reproduced in the *Todmorden Advertiser* at the time, Samuel Fielden was born at Todmorden, near Rochdale, Lancashire, in 1847, and was the son of a man who was prominent in the Chartist riots of 1848. 'He is a shaggy, unkempt man with a good deal of rough eloquence and has been one of the most intemperate of the anarchist orators. He came to this country [America] in 1868. Before that he had been a cotton operative, and his first employment in this country was at

[1] Dr. Paul Carus in *The Open Court*, vol. VIII (1894), p. 4080.

Oakton Community College
7900 North Nagle
Morton Grove Ill. 60053

a woollen mill in New Jersey. He afterwards worked at a farm at Summit, Illinois, and afterwards took to teaming in Chicago. Lately he has had a team of his own and worked for the Ernshaw–Nodenschatz stone company.'

An account of the 'Bomb Outrage', which appeared in the *Todmorden Advertiser* on 14 May 1886, reports, tendentiously, as follows:

Some two thousand anarchists assembled in Haymarket Square. They were not men on strike but professional agitators who had no real grievance but who were accustomed to indulge in wild oratory. Herr August Spies, the editor of the *Arbeiter Zeitung* (a local, German-language, Socialist weekly) was the first speaker, and he was followed by a man named Parsons. Neither of them was wilder than he had often previously been. Then Samuel Fielden mounted upon a barrel, and among other things said: 'The newspapers charged the Socialists with cowardice. They were there that night to repel that lie and prove that they were willing to risk their lives in the cause. . . . When the Capitalists were made to realise that it was unsafe for them to be in a place where labour was dissatisfied, that was the labourers' only hope. That day would come.' It was upon hearing these latter words that the constable made his report at the station. Soon afterwards a squad of policemen marched across the square in front of the speakers' stand. The effect was electrical. Parsons, pointing his hands menacingly at the police, was apparently about to denounce them, when the mob, forestalling his wishes, yelled out 'Kill them', 'Down with the police'. One correspondent states that Fielden shouted, 'To arms', when the police made their appearance. The men on the speakers' stand stamped and gesticulated: the mob hooted and cursed furiously. A bomb was then thrown from amongst the mob, another quickly followed, and then another, each bursting with a loud report alongside the squad of policemen. The effect was appalling. . . . One of the bombs was badly aimed and burst nearer the mob than the police, with the result that several civilians were either killed or wounded by their own friends. Tremendous excitement followed. The mob seemed determined to complete the work of destruction and appeared mad with passion. The police, enraged at the sight of their dead and mutilated comrades, drew their revolvers and fired recklessly right ahead. The mob promptly responded and a regular pistol fusillade began. The mob wavered, and then all of a sudden seemed to lose all cohesion, turned, and finally fled in a blind panic, strangely at variance with their previous determination and courage.

A later report, in the same newspaper, of the inquest which followed, includes the following statement by Fielden:

Last night when I got home from work, I saw in the [Chicago] *Daily News* that there was to be an important meeting of the American Group of Socialists, to which I belong, at the *Arbeiter Zeitung* office. I hurried down there . . . to discuss the question of calling meetings to organise

the sewing girls of the city. It was then that I learned of the meeting on
Haymarket Square and I was urged to go over there because Mr. Spies
was there alone. I consented to go over with Mr. Parsons and spoke as
you have heard.

Fielden then described the approach of the police and said that when
Captain Ward called on them to disperse, he remonstrated, saying it
was a peaceful meeting. Captain Ward repeated his order. Fielden then
dismounted from the wagon and, as he stepped down to the sidewalk,
he received a shot in the knee. Fielden said he had not the slightest idea
who threw the bombs and had no suspicion that there was a bomb in
the audience. He admitted that he had urged the people to throttle the
law, but he said: 'It looks very fierce to put it that way without one's
reasons for it. I am an anarchist. I admit that. I do not believe in
arbitrary authority but in voluntary association. I consider that arbitrary
authority is inimical to the best interest of human faculties.' The fore-
man then said, 'Did you ever talk about dynamite with Mr. Spies?'
'Oh, yes,' replied Fielden, 'we have talked about dynamite. Who has
not? We spoke of the assassination of the Czar, and the attempt to blow
up the House of Commons, or something like that.' At the close of the
inquiry the jury returned a verdict against Fielden as one of the aiders
and abettors of the person who threw the bombs.

It is perhaps necessary to add, before leaving the subject of Fielden,
that Clarence Darrow, later to become a famous criminal lawyer, who
was corporation lawyer to the city of Chicago at the time of the bombing
incident, gives a rather different version of what he understood had
happened in the Square: one much nearer to Fielden's account than to
that of the anonymous Chicago correspondent, and one most strongly
upheld by his very good friend, M. M. Trumbull, who knew Fielden
well. According to Darrow, a permit allowing the meeting to take place
had been granted by the authorities.

When the First of May had passed, with many threats of disturbance,
some of the citizens were fearing greater trouble (at the scheduled meeting on May 4th), so the Mayor, Carter Harrison Senior, went to the
Square and listened to what the speakers said. Sam Fielden, an Englishman, was speaking. The mayor then told the policeman the meeting
seemed to him to be all right, and started for home. No sooner had the
mayor disappeared than a company of policemen marched up to the
wagon and commanded the meeting to disperse. Fielden replied that
they were about to go home however. Thereupon a bomb was thrown
from an alley into the Square, which landed in the midst of the police,
killing seven and injuring about fifty.

Darrow concludes this section of his memoirs with these words:

It was but a very few years after the executions until the bar in general throughout the state and elsewhere, came to believe (largely through the ceaseless activity of the Amnesty Association led by General Trumbull) that the conviction was brought about through malice and hatred, and that the trial was unfair and the judgement of the court unsound, and that the opinion of the court was a standing menace to the liberty of the citizens. Eventually the men were pardoned. It is perfectly certain that he [Governor John P. Altgeld of Illinois] would not have saved them if he had not been satisfied that there was not sufficient evidence to connect them with the killing.[1]

Trumbull also served as a rallying point during these turbulent events for at least two other ex-Chartists as well as several English trade unionists, who had lain submerged beneath the surface of American life until his public stand over the injustice brought them quickly to his side. G. J. Harney, a Chartist leader of considerable influence still, and now resident in Boston, Massachusetts, started up a regular correspondence with Trumbull at this time,[2] remarking later that 'His name was not known to fame when [he was] a participant in our old movement, but [his] subsequent career has been such that every old Chartist still living may feel proud of their once humble, unknown associate.'[3] James Charlton, a Chartist mechanic from Newcastle formerly associated with T. A. Devyr and G. J. Harney, was also prompted to join the Amnesty Association after reading about Trumbull's stand. A lifelong friend of G. J. Holyoake, who frequently stayed with him in Chicago, he was now manager of the Chicago and Alton Railroad and resident in Chicago.[4] Even W. J. Linton, hearing that his American pupil Walter Crane, a friend of H. D. Lloyd, was going to Chicago to help with the Association, sent a message of support and 'a financial contribution'.[5] There were also contacts with the Association made by J. F. Bray, Richard Hinton and David Johnston.[6]

How far Trumbull had travelled politically by this time, is not absolutely clear. It is interesting to note, however, that in 1892 he added the following fiery postscript to his autobiographical sketch first

[1] Trumbull to Lloyd, 23 Feb. 1890, Henry D. Lloyd Papers, Wisc. State Historical Society. Also *Todmorden Advertiser*, 30 June, 1893: also Clarence Darrow, *The Story of My Life*, chap. III (1934).
[2] Harney Papers, Mrs. Frank Lees Black, Eugene, Oregon.
[3] *Open Court*, vol. IV, p. 2631.
[4] Schoyen, *op. cit.*, pp. 100, 226, 263.
[5] C. M. Destler, *Henry Demarest Lloyd and the Empire of Reform* (Philadelphia, 1963), p. 103.
[6] *Ibid.*, 104.

published in 1890, which is clearly far more concerned with the grim future facing the American workingman than it is with the exposure of Pinkerton:

In the days of my hot youth, I was a revolutionary Chartist, eager to fight for the overthrow of the British monarchy and the erection on its ruins of a British republic: and there were enough of those who aspired as I did to cause the Government alarm.

Among the prominent Chartists of the north was a young man whose name was Allan Pinkerton: and when the Government was busy fining, imprisoning and transporting Chartists, Pinkerton made his escape to the United States where, in bitter irony, grim fate made him establish the most dangerous order of spies that ever preyed upon social freedom in America: and it became his unlucky destiny to give his name to an army of illegal soldiers not under the command of the nation or the state, an impudent menace to liberty: an irresponsible brigade of hired banditti, equipped with rifles and threatening every American working man.[1]

But, while he was most insistent that he would never be prepared to go as far towards Socialism as his friend Thomas Morgan, there is no doubt that he had long since abandoned the strictly individualistic viewpoint he shared with Andrew Carnegie in the 1860's. Then he had believed that democracy meant only the equality of opportunity, not the equality of condition;[2] now he was less absolute: 'I believe in a communism of rights, privileges and opportunities, but not in a communism of their achievements and results.'[3] Trumbull had also rediscovered the deep sympathy in himself for the spirit of Morgan's activities at this time: 'American Chartism has a very close resemblance to the English article of that name, so close indeed, that listening to Mr. T. J. Morgan (on the public platform in Chicago) ... I thought myself once more a boy in London cheering the labor gospel at the Chartist hall in John Street. Mr. Morgan looked like a Chartist, spoke like a Chartist, and the spirit of Chartism was the magnetic string by which he tied his audience together.'[4] From this and from other hints contained in this article on Morgan, it would seem reasonable to assume that by this stage in his political evolution, Trumbull's prime concern was that of reconciling socialist planning with personal freedom. As he himself said at the close of his pamphlet on Jefferson: 'It may well be that the only difference between my socialist friends and myself is on the question, How much personal freedom will the citizen have?'[5] In

---

[1] *Open Court*, vol. VI (1892), p. 3316.
[2] *Jefferson, op. cit.*, p. 14.   [3] *Ibid.*, p. 15.
[4] *Wheelbarrow, op. cit.*, p. 198.
[5] *Jefferson, op. cit.*, p. 14.

this dilemma Trumbull was in very good company on both sides of the Atlantic and his question prompts the thought that, if he had lived longer, he would have found himself much in the same position that G. D. H. Cole found himself—inclined towards a type of Guild socialist pluralism but completely opposed to any form of centralism.

8

Conclusion

A variety of contributory causes effected the decline of Chartist agitation after the rejection of the second petition in May 1842. Trade revival; well-subsidized plans of emigration; the rapid expansion of mining and railway construction; the Anti-Corn Law League; the militancy of the middle class; the removal of the key agitators from many districts—all these and more, can and should be listed. But it often seems as though the most obviously effective cause, the decapitation of the movement by dispersing its leaders, has become hidden from view and therefore underrated, in favour of economic causes. Admittedly, there are generally more important developments to be found in the working of economic forces than there are in the efforts of individuals or even groups. Even so, the dispersal factor is worthy of a much closer examination than it has received hitherto, since it can now be argued that the permanent loss overseas of so many vigorous working-class leaders, affected not merely the immediate Chartist agitation but also the general development of the British labour movement for the next forty years.

In round, and necessarily approximate numbers, those Chartists who left the UK for the USA between 1839 and 1860 cannot have been more than 500, as we have seen.[1] Moreover, they were obviously not a representative sample of the society they left behind. Migration, even involuntary migration, being a selective process, those who left were bound to be among the most impatient, the most dynamic and activist elements of the working-class leadership. Certainly the 70 Chartists studied here confirm this view—and there must be more still to be reckoned with. Men like William Ashton, John (the Fifer) Rees, John Rewcastle, William Rider, Thomas Devyr, Peter Bussey, Richard Mellor and W. Butterworth—even Allan Pinkerton, the 'turncoat' who

---

[1] See Chapter 3, p. 35.

became 'one of the most hated men in the American labour movement'[1]
—were determined men. All of these were, of course, 'physical force'
Chartists with the authorities hard on their heels towards the end. But
they left behind them many more of the 'conservative', passive and long-
suffering of their comrades than they took with them. Indeed, not one
of the emigres studied here was without some distinctive individuality
—though perhaps that is one of the first requirements of any radical
leader—and few were without resourcefulness when things went against
them economically. For example, according to J. D. Borthwick who met
several ex-Chartists in California after 1848 (but omits to give a single
name), they were less confined than most immigrants to one speciality.
This, he said, 'made them better men (than most English mechanics
and workmen he had met) to be turned adrift in a new country where
they may well have to employ themselves in a hundred different ways
before they find an opportunity of following the trade to which they
have been brought up'.[2]

Even those 'moral force' Chartists, men such as Bray, Trumbull,
Charlton, Dealtry, and Tinker for whom Chartism had declined into
mere O'Connorism by the time they emigrated to take their political
views to a newer and better environment: even they refused to be dis-
solved in the melting-pot of American society. In fact, they were very
careful to remain critical, militant and self-consciously working class in
outlook, while wearing American middle-class 'disguises'. Take Trumbull for example: he joined the army early in 1847 to escape from
'humping barrels of pork in a Boston pork warehouse for a dollar a day',
and his dreams of becoming a radical lawyer had therefore to be
postponed until he reached Iowa in 1853. In the meantime:

Through military association I became well acquainted with many of
the men who afterwards became famous as generals fighting against each
other in the Civil War. Of course I knew nothing at the time of the ethics
or the politics of the war with Mexico: but afterwards, when I came to
study the genius and the inspiration of it, I thought it nothing at all to
be proud of.[3]

This is no vainglorious militarist speaking; nor even simply a cynical
opportunist: rather, here speaks a thinking radical. And even after the
Civil War, when through bravery as well as ability he has reached the
lofty rank of general, his critical sense is as keen as ever:

[1] M. M. Trumbull writing in *The Open Court*, vol. VI (1892), p. 3316.
[2] J. D. Borthwick, *Three Years in California* (Edinburgh, 1857), p. 310.
[3] Matthew M. Trumbull, 'Aristocracy in America', *Nineteenth Century*,
vol. 18, Aug. 1885, pp. 209–17.

It is commonly believed by many Americans that, because they have no titled nobility, nor any hereditary privileged orders, that therefore they have no aristocracy: this is a mistake. Aristocracy is not only legal in the United States but it has been deliberately established in the Constitution . . . by which I mean 'aristocracy' as the Americans use the word, namely to describe a class of pretenders who would be titled people if they could, and a class who assume superior importance on account of money. . . . The Toryism of the American Supreme Court would comfort the soul of Lord Eldon. . . .[1]

Here is a veritable Cobbett speaking, in a hard-hitting article which could find no editorial acceptance in America but which was printed gleefully in England as 'the eccentric viewpoint of an American general'. By the side of this reasoned piece, Harney's comments about America, in letters to Engels, roughly about the same time, are mere mumblings: 'I am sorry to know that the Avelings are going to America. Pray urge caution upon them. After all the brag and bunkum, England is the land of true liberty. . . . In my judgement, Dr. and Mrs. Aveling had better leave well alone and stay where they are.' Again, on 6 May 1887, Harney wrote to Engels as follows:

I by no means take your favourable view of the Knights of Labour and similar [American] organisations. In the first place their puerilities disgust me. Their 'dignities' make me feel sea-sick. Vanity and love of notoriety are at the foundation of all these societies and organisations. A lot of fellows want to be Grand this and Grand that: Grand Dictator, Grand Chaplain, Grand Doorkeeper, Grand Pisspot-emptier, Almighty Grand Panjandrum etc. etc. A Yankee 'Sir Knight' makes me feel that I could—well, not need an emetic! Then my idea of these fellows is that they aim at establishing an Aristocracy of Labour, in fact playing the role of that gang in London who are represented in Parliament by Broadhurst, Howell and Co., well held up by you to scorn.[2]

John Francis Bray, on the other hand, largely because he was alone in having some real knowledge of American democracy in advance of his emigration (being American-born), ploughed his solitary socialist furrow from 1842 to his death in 1897, preferring to stay out of the mainstream of the American labour movement for most of his life, but eventually earning the following respectful paragraph from the editor of the *Detroit Echo* in 1885:

In the national Greenback labor convention in Chicago in June, 1880, at which 44 Socialist delegates were admitted, had they been allowed

[1] Matthew M. Trumbull, 'Aristocracy in America', *Nineteenth Century*, vol. 18, Aug. 1885, pp. 209–17.
[2] Marx–Engels Archives, International Institut voor Sociale Geschiedenis, Amsterdam, catalogue L IV 200.

to vote for a nominee for President (of the United States), they would have voted solidly for John F. Bray, who is thought to be the oldest living Socialist born in the US.

Clearly, Bray, like Harney and Trumbull, never lost sight of his youthful dream during his long years in America, though he confesses he came near to despair at times. Again like his two comrades-in-arms,

he remained a youth as long as he lived, youthful in his enthusiasm for the ideals of humanity, youthful in his combative disposition, and youthful in the spirit with which he wielded his pen, always sprightly, always brisk and quick in his thrusts and repartees. . . . But back of the sarcasm of his caustic pen, there was always the good heart of a sympathetic nature and an unshaken confidence in the final victory of truth and justice.[1]

Remarkably, almost all of the subjects in this study whose dates are known with certainty (Barker, Bray, Burn, Campbell, Charlton, Cluer, Denton, Devyr, Fraser, Harney, Holyoake, Johnston, Linton, Pinkerton, Trevellick and Trumbull), lived long and very active lives, several being referred to as 'very youthful' old men when they died. Now there is surely more to their continuing vitality than can be accounted for simply by the comforts of 'the American way of life'. Few of them were comfortably off, except for short periods: only consider the readiness with which Devyr spent his 'small (property) fortune' on the financing of short-lived radical newspapers. (Pinkerton was the exception here, as in so many other ways.) More important perhaps, Chartist emigres usually saw themselves as 'marked' men, and even in some cases 'chosen' men, after they had been some time in America, and they never lost the view that America was the only land remaining where radical change was still possible, given the right (English) sort of organization behind it.

In England the whole duty of man, as set down in the workingman's catechism, is to find out upon how little he can live. In America the workingman sets himself to find out how much he ought to have to live upon, equitably compared with what falls to other classes. He does not see exactly how to get it when he has found out the amount. But it is the attitude that is important.

Thus wrote G. J. Holyoake in 1880 while he was the house-guest in Chicago of his ex-Chartist friend from Newcastle, James Charlton, 'of the Chicago and Alton railway'.[2] He saw as clearly as any of his many

---

[1] Dr. Paul Carus, Funeral Oration, Trumbull Supplement, *Open Court*.
[2] G. J. Holyoake, *Among the Americans* (Chicago, 1881), pp. 214-18.

G

ex-Chartist friends in America that it was this attitude of equality with one's fellow man which must be strenuously encouraged, 'lest the crippling chains of English deference fall upon the American working-man'.

Perhaps most important of all therefore, Chartists in America viewed themselves primarily as missionaries. Even the avowed secularists among them possessed an undeniable religiosity; they felt a responsibility to their God to liberate workingmen everywhere; they believed that they were under a deep moral obligation to do so, and never admitted that their zeal should be contained within particular national boundaries. When Daniel Weaver, for example, wanted to stress the need for unity within his union, this ex-Chartist founder of the American Miners' Association phrased his words like a preacher: 'One of America's immortals has said, "To me there is no East, no West, no North, no South"; and I would say, Let there be no English, no Irish, Germans, Scotch or Welsh. We are just all workers together.'[1]

Embattled men, all too often treated like pariahs, they seemed to derive their exaltation from the wellsprings of their own righteousness. They were completely sure of themselves and of the efficacy of their programmes of reform. And it is hardly surprising, therefore, that the arrival in the USA of such a breed of men prompted certain conservative editorialists in cities like Boston and Philadelphia, to write of 'this mania that is abroad . . . and spreading far and wide'. Americans were convinced it was part of an international conspiracy to subvert American democracy. It had 'commenced in England' and had as its objects the overthrow of sound government and property.[2]

But this fairly predictable reaction on the part of American Conservatives, pales into historical insignificance at the side of the hopeless collapse following the departure of Chartist leaders, on the part of the leaderless masses in Britain. This widespread apathy and sudden indifference to Chartist politics has never been adequately explained, though it was vividly described in a letter written to Ernest Jones at the end of the 'fifties. The writer, John Snowdon, was a former militant of the Halifax Chartist Association, and he was answering an appeal that Jones had made for funds:

I am sorry to inform you that there is no Chartist organization in Halifax nor in any of the numerous villages surrounding it. . . . Many of those

---

[1] Quoted by E. A. Wieck in *The American Miners' Assoc.* (New York, 1940), p. 85.
[2] *Boston Daily Transcript*, 12 April 1853.

that were once active Chartists have emigrated. And others, though residing here as usual, have become so thoroughly disgusted at the indifference and utter inattention of the multitude to their best interests that they too are resolved to make no more sacrifices in a public cause.[1]

For a brief moment there had seemed to be some light at the end of the tunnel, especially for the unskilled workers. Then suddenly it was all black and more hopeless than ever. But the question arises, why was the struggle abandoned so readily? Economic reasons, while they help to put their attitude into perspective, do not entirely explain it. Britain was undoubtedly entering upon an era of industrial monopoly that was to be effectively challenged only from the mid-'seventies. More important, however, it was the skilled workers alone who were capable of taking advantage of the new possibilities of strength through trade union organization at this time. The unskilled masses, hardly touched by unionism for forty years after the collapse of the Grand National in 1834, and enduring living standards which stayed ever the same during a period of unprecedented prosperity, remained utterly passive and indifferent. Again, why? The answer would seem to be, partly because they suffered no absolute reduction in their standard of life,[2] and in consequence could not easily 'stoke up' their own class consciousness; but also because there was no longer any united body of working-class agitators stimulating them into some kind of political activity and forcing them to correct their retarded theoretical development. In other words, the dispersal of almost the entire Chartist leadership, some overseas but most to prison, not only affected the immediate programme of political reform; it also brought about the shelving of all further self-reliant political activity on the part of the workingman for the next generation. This, of course, ensured that middle-class leadership took over from the Chartists and that the central fact of bourgeois society—the exploitation of wage labour by capital—was increasingly lost sight of through a concern over 'Free Trade in Land'. The direct loss through emigration of so many of the most vigorous and intelligent of the Chartist rank-and-file was therefore Britain's loss and America's gain. It was Britain's loss, not merely because of the long interruption which the failure of Chartism caused in radical thinking about social democracy, but also because, by the end of the 1880's and largely through the organizing ability of ex-Chartist

---

[1] Letter dated 16 October 1859, Chetham's Library, Manchester.
[2] See B. R. Mitchell and P. Deane. *Abstract of British Historical Statistics* (Cambridge, 1962), pp. 343–44.

trade unionists like John Siney and Robert Hinchcliffe, the political organization of the working class in America was, for a brief period, more complete and more effective than that of the British workers.

It was America's gain, also, and not merely in the areas of land reform and labour unionization. Most of the Chartist emigres were single men in their early thirties, most had been weavers by trade, nearly all were urbanites, and most had been Chartist lecturers and therefore influential local leaders. Five had been Methodist preachers, out of the seventy proven Chartists specifically catalogued in this study,[1] three had been schoolmasters, seven printers and/or journalists, two tailors and five joiners. Most had left towns and cities in the north of England and settled for several years at least, in the four main cities on the eastern seaboard of America. Most popular cities for their settlements were New York and Boston, where tiny 'villages' of ex-Chartists were set up and lasted longer than would have been expected among such strong individualists; nine, however, settled separately in Chicago, five in Philadelphia and three in Pittsburgh. Four entered the US through the port of Galveston direct from England; Wisconsin, Kansas and Iowa welcomed five Chartists at least, between 1840 and 1850; only one is reported to have gone to the Far West following the discovery of gold in 1849, but at least four were travelling that way when last seen.

Reasonably complete demographic data is only available on fifty of the seventy, but the ages of these ranged from nineteen to fifty-six years. Upon first arrival in America, three persons were still in their teens, six in their twenties, thirty-three in their thirties, ten in their forties and four in their fifties. The total time spent per man in the US varied from two months (John Alexander) to fifty-five years (John Bray). Four remained in America for less than one year, nine from two to three years, ten from five to ten years, six from ten to twenty years, and two for over twenty years before returning home. Even so, at least thirty ended their lives in the US, several making brief trips back home only after they had really established themselves in their new country.

For those who saw Chartism as primarily 'a knife and fork question', such as ex-nailmakers like Chatterton and ex-weavers like Bussey and Ashton—America was judged largely by its economic opportunities. When these fell short of expectation, they would be likely to start dreaming of a bygone age of Tory or 'Feudal socialism', as did Brothers, and Bussey after him. On the other hand, mature, 'Mazzinian' republicans like G. J. Harney and W. J. Linton made no attempt to enter the

[1] Appendix A for full list.

American labour world, going in on themselves and their memories. Irishmen like Campbell and Devyr never ceased to be Irishmen, became men of property as soon as they could afford to, and seemed to become slightly unbalanced in later life, possibly due to their unlimited appetite for political intrigue and agitation. Trade unionists like Siney, Weaver, Smith and Macpherson found it easy as well as advantageous to become Americans. The same could be said of Trumbull and Charlton, both of whom disappeared into the professional class until they felt called upon to emerge and identify themselves during the Anarchist trials of 1886, that shocked liberals everywhere as well as socialists. Many other Chartists, one suspects, refused to stay within the ranks of labour. Many found jumping to the other side of the fence much easier in America and took advantage of it. Trade unionists and socialists like T. J. Morgan and Richard Hinton thought nothing of owning city property and running small businesses along with their union activities;[1] while Macpherson and Harney mixed only with the leading citizens in their respective abodes of Springdale, Wisconsin, and Boston, Mass. Nevertheless, as a type they were in bold contrast to the run of British–American workingmen, with their cautious unionism and their limited economic aims. They would usually fight for the mass of labourers rather than for their own immediate welfare as skilled craftsmen and never tired of urging working-class solidarity, which was their common message. In conclusion, while they may have been but a very tiny fraction of the massive flow of immigration into the US from 1840–60, they were a most creative minority and had a strikingly catalystic effect on the whole American labour movement, which was out of all proportion to their total numbers.

[1] Yearley, *op. cit.*, p. 314.

Appendix A

Who was who

Notes on 76 British Chartists (and Chartist children) in America[1]

Aitken, William: Born 1814, Dunbar, Scot., weaver. Moved to Ashton-u-Lyne, Lancs., became schoolmaster and 'physical force' Chartist. Contacted by Mormons. Left UK 1842 for Nauvoo, Ill., USA, where there was a community of Icarian or Cabetite communists as well as Mormons. Left for home after violence broke out in community. Author of *A Journey up the Mississippi River from the north to Nauvoo, city of Latter Day Saints* (Ashton, 1845). Elected Grand Master of Oddfellows in Lancs. 1846. Believed to have been a paid agent of Southern Confederacy during Civil War. Died (suicide ?) in Ashton, 1869.

Alexander, John: Born 1808, Mauchline, Ayrshire, Scot., a joiner by trade; moved to London in 1830's. O'Brienite Chartist and close personal friend of O'Brien. Left UK in 1848 'with a whole shipload of Chartists', for Houston, Texas, hoping to found a Cabetite communist community. Member, with John Ellis, of North Texas Colonization Company. Wrote commissioned letters for O'Brien's newspaper, *The Reformer*, May 1849. Returned to England, 'disgusted', in 1849. Believed to have died in 1872. (Shepperson.)

Ashton, William: Born 1806, Silkstone, nr. Barnsley, Yorks. Linen weaver. Transported to Australia in 1830, liberated 1838 (fare home paid by Barnsley weavers) became prominent Barnsley Chartist ('physical force') leader; friend of Peter Bussey, George White and O'Connor . . . until the Newport rising when he quarrelled violently with O'Connor. Arrested and charged with conspiracy, York Assizes, July 1840. Left UK 1842. Lived near Bussey in New York City. Died in Yorks. ?

Astin, James: Born 1806, Padiham, Burnley, Lancs., millworker. 'Very active' Chartist, 'physical force', arrested twice before he was forced to leave UK 'in a hurry', 1848. Went to work in cotton mill in Fall River, Mass. Oddfellows paid the fares for his wife and family to follow him there. Believed to have returned home in 1850's.

[1] Of this figure, only the first 70 seem to qualify as Chartists; the remainder, however, were proud sons of prominent Chartists and made a point of mentioning this connection in their writings.

Bairstow, Jonathan: Born 1822, Leicester (?), handloom weaver and Chartist lecturer in Leicester, 1841–46. Acc. to Gammage (p. 402) he left UK in 1853 with Peter M. McDouall for New York. But acc. to Harney, he was drowned in *The President* shipwreck off the coast of Australia, 1853.

Barker, Joseph: Born 1806, Wortley, nr. Leeds, Yorks. Wool-spinner and Methodist preacher. 'Moral force' Chartist, Temperance Movt. Abolitionist. Author of *The People* (Wortley, 1848–69) and *The Liberators* (Wortley, 1852–53). Left UK for Boston, Mass., and Omaha, Nebraska, 1851, to join farmer-brother. In the US 1851–60, and again 1865 to his death in 1875 in Nebraska.

Bates, John: Born 1809 in Yorks., coal miner and Chartist. Left UK in 1848 for New York, and Pittsburgh, Pennsylvania. Founder in 1848/49, 'on Chartist principles', of first mine union in America.

Bower, Robert: Born 1807 in Lancs. Weaver and 'physical force' Chartist. Left UK 1848 for Lawrence, Mass. Became 'most important labour leader in Lawrence' up to and just after Civil War (Foner).

Bray, John Francis: Born 1809, Washington, DC, of English parents. Went with father to Leeds, Yorks., at age of 13. Became a printer. Trade union organizer in Leeds, 1829. 'Moral force' Chartist. Author *Labour's Wrongs* (1838); *A Voyage from Utopia* (1839); *American Destiny* (1864); *God and Man, a Unity* (1879). Visited France, 1842. Left UK for Boston, Mass., 1842, to join brother. Married and went to farm in Pontiac, Michigan. Printer and trade unionist in Detroit, Mich., till his death in 1897. Described after his death as 'the Grand Old Man of American Socialism'.

Brown, William: Born 1801. Leeds, Yorks., cloth finisher and 'physical force' Chartist. Left UK 1841 for New York City and Cleveland, Ohio. Author of *America: Four Years' Residence in the US & Canada* (Leeds, 1849). Criticized all things American, especially education. Met Bussey 'down on his luck' in New York, just before he returned home.

Brown, William S.: Born 1812, Glasgow; printer/preacher. 'Moral force' secretary of Glasgow Charter Assoc. Left UK 1850 for Boston, Mass. 'Returned home to die', 1875 (?)

Burn, James Dawson: Born 1806, Glasgow. Weaver and 'physical force' Chartist. Grand Master of Oddfellows. Moved to London in 1850's. Author of *The Autobiography of a Beggar Boy* (London, 1855). Left UK for New York City and Newark, NJ, 1862. Feted by press 'and then left to starve'. Worked in Federal munitions factory: wrote *Three Years among the Working Classes in the US during the War* (London, 1865). Returned to London. Wrote a novel, *The Beggar Boy* (London, 1882).

Bussey, Peter: Born Bedale, Yorks., 1805, Weaver/publican, Bradford, Yorks., 'physical force' member of 1839 Chartist Convention. Left UK 1839, 'in a hurry', after abortive Newport rising in which he was implicated, for New York City and Fall River, Mass. Ran a Chartist boarding house in New York. Tried farming and failed. Tried newspaper editing and failed. Barrow boy in New York, acc. to William Brown. Returned home in 1854, 'a Tory'. Died 1869.

Butterworth, William: Born 1808, Oldham, Lancs., weaver and 'well known Chartist in Lancashire and Yorkshire'. 'Physical force'; in Liverpool prison, 1840–41, for 'promoting rebellion'; left UK 1842. Stayed with Bussey for a time. Returned home.

Campbell, John: Born 1810 in Ireland; weaver in Manchester, 1840. 'Physical force' Chartist; Secretary, National Chartist Association, 1841. Protege of Abel Heywood with whom he lived briefly in Manchester and thus learned about radical book publishing; left UK 'hurriedly' 1843, for Philadelphia. Secretary/founder of Social Reform Society, 1844. Became prominent in Philadelphia book circles. Author of *A Theory of Equality: or the way to make every Man act honestly* (Philadelphia, 1848); and *Negro-Mania* (Philadelphia, 1851). Died in Philadelphia, 1874.

Carnegie, William: Born 1801, Dunfermline, Scot. (father of Andrew Carnegie); hand-loom weaver, 'moral force' Chartist, secretary of local Chartist Association. Close friend of John Fraser. Wrote articles for Cobbett's *Political Register*, and letters in Chartist newspaper, *The True Scotsman*, July 1838. Left UK 1848 'on the proceeds from the sale of his four hand-looms', for Pittsburgh, Pennsylvania. Died 1872.

Carpenter, William: Born 1797, London, printer/editor. 'Unstamped press' agitator, later a 'moral force' Chartist. Editor of *The Charter*, 1839–40. Left UK for New York in 1850's. Returned home after short stay, 'with hard luck stories for the London press'. Died London, 1874.

Charlton, James: Born 1820, Newcastle-on-Tyne; miner, later engineer/mechanic. Social Democrat member of Northern Political Union; 'physical force' Chartist; close friend of Thomas Devyr, Holyoake and Harney. Left UK 1855 for Chicago, Ill. Manager of Chicago–Alton Railroad in 1870 (secured free rail pass for Holyoake when H. stayed with him in Chicago in 1880's). Revealed his Chartist past to Trumbull after Haymarket Riots of 1886, and made contribution to Amnesty Association. Still alive in 1897 when he wrote two letters to Mrs. Theophilia Campbell, daughter of Richard Carlile, about his friendship with Holyoake. (See R. Carlile Coll., Huntington Lib., San Marino, California.)

Chatterton, George (?): Born 1804, Sheffield; nailmaker; 'physical force' Chartist; Secretary of the Sheffield Working Men's Association. Left UK 1839 with Wolstenholme 'and twelve other men from the local staple trades . . . to escape arrest' (*Sheffield Mercury*, 5 Oct. 1839) to join other Sheffield workers in Westport, Conn. Believed to have returned home in 1850's.

Cluer, John C.: Born 1806, Glasgow, weaver, 'forceful local Chartist leader'. Left UK 1839 for New York City and Lowell, Mass. Became member of the National Reform Movement, and a prime mover in the New York Ten Hours Movement. Died 1886, Boston, Mass.

Dealtry, William: Born 1817, Bristol; cabinet maker; Chartist (?). Left UK 1847 for Albany, NY, and Cincinnati, Ohio. Author of *Money: Its History, Evils and Remedy* (Albany, 1858) and, *The Laborer: A Remedy for his Wrongs* (Cincinnati, 1869.)

Deegan, John: Born ? Ireland, a weaver in Hyde and Glossop area; Chartist representative for Hyde at first convention. A 'physical force' man, he was 'tried' by fellow Chartists for speaking against *Northern Star* policy (i.e. against O'Connor). Left UK 1841 for Boston, Mass.

Denton, William: Born 1823, Bristol; a weaver and later a Chartist lecturer in London. Wrote articles on phrenology. Left UK 1842 for New York City where he became a prominent anti-slavery agitator. Later converted to spiritualism. Visited Australia 1883 and died there.

Devyr, Thomas Ainge: Born 1805, Donegal, Ireland, pedlar, author, *Our Natural Rights* (Belfast, 1836; republished New York, 1842); went to London and became a special constable while trying to be a journalist; Assistant Editor, *Northern Liberator*, 1839–40, Newcastle-on Tyne; Corresponding Secretary of Northern Political Union; organizer of an armed band of Chartist guerillas which almost went into action. Left UK, a 'wanted man', 1840, for New York City. Given editorship of a Democrat newspaper in Williamsburg, NY. Sacked after criticizing the party line. Became organizer, Anti-Rent Party, in Upstate New York; also member of the National Reform Party in NY. Moved to Brooklyn. Edited a Fenian newspaper, *The Irish People*, from 1865–66. Articles in *Northern Star, New York Tribune* and *Irish World*; author of *The Odd Book, or Chivalry in Modern Days* (New York, 1882). Died 1887, Brooklyn, NY.

Dillon, James: Born 1824, Stockport, Cheshire. Shoemaker and Chartist(?). Left UK 1845 for Lynn, Mass. Vice-President, Lynn Mechanics' Association, 1859. (Yearley.)

Duncan, Abram: Born 1798, Glasgow. Woodturner and trade union spokesman. Chartist pastor in Arbroath. Left UK 1848 for Boston, Mass. Returned home after prolonged musical tour of Eastern cities. (He and his daughter had a popular music-hall act.)

Fraser, John: Born 1794, Johnstone, nr. Glasgow. Schoolmaster/ journalist. Founded Edinburgh Radical Association, 1836; member Edinburgh Technical Association, advocate of Hygeism, reported trial of Glasgow Cotton Spinners for *Northern Star* (Jan. 1838); editor, *The True Scotsman*, a Scottish Chartist paper. Left UK 1848 for Boston, Mass. Believed to have returned home in 1870. Died 1879.

Harney, George Julian: Born 1817, Deptford, London. Cabin boy, pot boy, shop boy in Hetherington's shop, Chartist lecturer, leading national figure, and journalist. Social Democrat Chartist. Editor, *Democratic Review* (1849–50). Moved to Jersey. Left UK 1863 for Boston, Mass. Returned home 1888. Wrote regular column for *Newcastle Chronicle* till his death, 1897.

Hinchcliffe, John: Born 1822, Bradford, Yorks. Tailor and active Chartist, says he knew Bussey and White 'well'; left UK 1847 for New York, then to Philadelphia, and then to St. Louis where he became a miner's lawyer. Settled in Belleville, Ill., 1860. Edited *Weekly Miner*; he joined American Miners' Association, 1860 'even though not a miner'. Died St. Louis, 1878.

Hinchcliffe, Robert: Born Bradford, 1817, brother of John and later associate of Robert Bower. Weaver and Chartist; left UK 1847 for Boston and Lawrence, Mass. Edited a workingmen's journal in Lawrence, on behalf of other Bradford weaver-emigrants.

Hinton, Richard: Born 1826, Lancs., weaver and Chartist. Left UK 1848 for Boston, Mass.; radical Republican Abolitionist and associate of John Brown; Colonel in Civil War; became 'a confirmed Socialist' after the war and correspondent for *Boston Weekly Voice*. Author, *English Radical Leaders* (New York, 1857).

Holyoake, George Jacob: Born 1817, Birmingham. Foundry-worker, Chartist lecturer, journalist, Co-operator and Secularist; for writings, see Bibliography; in prison 1841–43, left UK for New York, 1848; met Devyr in company of Horace Greeley; also visited Boston and Chicago on various visits to US after this, each time seeking out ex-Chartists. Intended to write definitive history of Chartism. Died London, 1906.

Johnston, David: Born 1803, Haddington, East Lothian, Scot. Weaver, then apprentice baker in Edinburgh and Camberwell, London. Married a Soho baker's daughter and, with her dowry, bought a baker's shop in Camberwell, South London; elected Overseer of the Poor in St. Giles, Camberwell, 1831, 'by popular vote'; 'was a keen (moral force) Chartist until rowdies from Kennington wrecked my shop in 1848'. Left UK 1848 for Chicago, Ill., after labouring work in New York and Philadelphia. Lived and worked in Chicago till 1890, when he died on trip to San Francisco. Author of *Autobiographical Reminiscences of an Octogenarian Scotchman* (Chicago, 1885).

Keen, Charles: Born 1816, East End, London. Dock worker and potman, friend and 'lieutenant' of Harney, member of Society of Fraternal Democrats; left UK 1848 for New York City but saw his 'future out on the western prairies'; seen in Kansas City, may have gone out later to Montana. Wrote letters to *Northern Star* (Feb. and April 1850).

Linton, W. J.: Born 1812, Bloomsbury, London. Engraver (described by Vizetelly, p. 119, vol. I., as 'the first wood engraver of his epoch . . . the future friend of Mazzini and other advanced liberals, at a time when to know them even was regarded as a crime'); 'moral force' Chartist; retired to Windermere, Westmorland, after 1848. Left UK 1866 for Boston, Mass. Met Harney. Settled in New Hampden, Conn. Went out to Montana briefly to organize British Colony of Republicans (i.e. Mazzinians); made contact with Chicago Amnesty Association in 1887 through his American pupil, Walter Crane. Died in US 1898. Author, *Three Score Years and Ten* (New York, 1894).

Lloyd, Thomas: Born 1824 in Staffordshire. Miner; emigrated to US 1860, 'formerly a very active Chartist'; went straight out to Illinois and active in labour movement, in and around mining town of Belleville, where he died in 1896. Friend and associate of Daniel Weaver.

Lowery, Robert: Born 1805, Newcastle-on-Tyne; tailor; leading Chartist ('moral force') in Newcastle, Temperance leader; member of Northern Political Union; left UK to join daughter and her Chartist husband, 1862, worked for a time in New York and Boston, Mass. Died Canada, 1863.

McDouall, Peter Murray: Born 1814, Newton Stewart, Scot. Moved to Ashton-u-Lyne, Lancs., at an early age; 'Doctor'/surgeon, Chartist lecturer and journalist (regular correspondent for *Northern Star*); several mysterious departures from Ashton when 'wanted'; visited France in 1840's; returned, stood trial, imprisoned, Chartist collection made for him when found starving in Ashton in 1850; said by Gammage to have gone to US with Bairstow in 1853 but more probably went only to Australia; believed drowned in *The President* shipwreck off coast of Australia, 1853. (Harney, *Newcastle Chronicle*.)

MacFarlane, Robert: Born 1801, Glasgow. Dyer, knew Allan Pinkerton 'when he was on our side', possibly a Chartist, left UK 1842 for New York, worked in Buffalo and Albany. Founded Mechanics' Mutual Protection Society in Albany, 1845, which lasted till 1848. Died in Brooklyn, 1865. (Yearley and Foner.)

MacPherson, James: Born 1817, Dundee, Scot., flax dresser, Scottish delegate to Chartist Convention, 1842; left UK 1848, settled in Springdale, Wisconsin; became Postmaster, JP, attorney. Died in Wisconsin.

Mann, James: Born 1812, Huddersfield, Yorks., weaver and 'moral force' Chartist, described as 'co-operative pioneer'; first chairman of Hebden Bridge 'American Society'; left UK for US, 1846, believed bound for Iowa/Wisconsin.

Mason, John: Born 1809, Newcastle-on-Tyne; printer and chairman, Northern Political Union. Good friend of Devyr, Rewcastle and Lowery. Left UK for New York, 1842.

Mellor, Richard: Born 1801, Stockport, Cheshire; weaver and 'Chartist who had to leave England in a hurry', 1839. Ran a boarding house in Galveston, Texas, 'which housed many men on the run, including Englishmen, before they headed out West'. (Michael Brook & Shepperson.)

Mitchell, John: Born 1810, Dundee. Weaver, founder member of Dundee Democratic Society, believed to have written Chartist poetry, friend of poet William Thom, and leader of the Chartist 'army' march on Forfar; left UK 1842, a 'wanted' man, bound for New York. (See '*Scottish Chartism*'.)

Mitchell, Thomas: Born 1809, Huddersfield, Yorks., weaver, friend of James Mann and member of Hebden Bridge Chartist American Society; founder of Bacup Co-op, 1845; left UK 1846, believed bound for Iowa/Wisconsin.

Pinkerton, Allan: Born 1819, Glasgow. Son of a policeman (?), power-loom dresser and 'physical force' Chartist, founder of Glasgow Democratic Club (an O'Connorite club); left UK 'in a hurry', 1842, went to Rockford, Ill., then Chicago. Visited by Pitkeithly in Chicago, Aug. 1842; helped farmers reclaim 'lost' cattle; started detective agency which later became famous. Author, *The Molly Maguires and the Detectives* (New York, 1877). Died, 1884.

Pitkeithly, Lawrence: Born 1801, Huddersfield, Yorks., weaver, 'physical force' Chartist following his work in Ten Hours Movement, delegate to Naitonal Chartist Association meeting in Manchester,

July, 1840. Wrote to Dr. John Smyles (relative of Samuel Smiles), a former English Radical resident in Rochester, NY, about prospects in America; left UK 1842 for New York, contacted Bussey (and Devyr?) and Smyles, moved on to Milwaukee, Wis., and met Pinkerton in Chicago, Ill. Wrote articles on his trip in *Northern Star*, returned home, 1843; died Manchester, 1858.

Powell, Thomas: Born 1805, Newtown, Wales; moved to London after youth as ironmonger's assistant, worked for Hetherington and became bookseller himself; Chartist missionary in Wales in 1840's; took party of English 'political' emigrants to South America (San Salvador) via New York where he worked briefly. Died 1850 in Trinidad. (For possible Chartist influence on constitution of San Salvador, see J. West.)

Proudfoot, James: Born 1812, Glasgow grain dealer, friend of O'Connor, president of Glasgow USA, 1838–40, helped to form Glasgow Charter Association, May 1842. Left UK 1844, settled in Boston, Mass.

Pyne, James T.: Born 1804, Newcastle-on-Tyne, picture frame maker. Left UK 1839, first reported in Albany, NY, 1840, as member of National Reform Association and associate of Thomas Devyr and Herefordshire-born George Evans. Devyr refers to him as an old campaigner in the cause. Possibly a Chartist.

Rees, John: Born 1810, Newport, Mon., mason, 'commonly called Jack the Fifer, mason, of Tredegar iron-works' (acc. to Wanted poster, dated Newport, Mon., 7 Nov. 1839), left UK 1839 with £100 reward on his head as one of the leaders of the Newport rising. Wrote home from Virginia, 1844, asking for news of his (captured) friend Jones, shortly before 'leaving to join the army of Texas'.

Rewcastle (or Rucastle), John: Born 1806, Newcastle-on-Tyne, druggist's assistant, prominent 'physical force' Chartist after being an anti-Poor Law agitator, knew Lowery and Pitkeithly, close friend of Devyr with whom he fled the UK 1840 for New York. Lived and worked for several years close to Peter Bussey and Ben Worswick.

Rider, William: Born 1817, Leeds, Yorks., stuff-weaver, printer's devil. Secretary, Radical Political Union, author *The Demagogue* (Leeds, 1834), member of Leeds Working Men's Association. Arrested and imprisoned. Left UK 1855, stayed at Bussey's Boarding House (taken over by Ben Worswick) in New York. Returned home 'after twenty years in America', acc. to letter received by Gammage, 1890 (Gammage, p. 414).

Roberts, Samuel: Born 1800, Llanbrymair, Montgomery. Congregational preacher and labour agitator, possibly a Chartist, contributed to *Y Chronicl*, a journal in Welsh, 1843, urging land reform and emigration, referred to landowners as thieves, Russian barons and barefaced robbers. Imprisoned. Left UK 1857 for Huntsville, Tennessee; returned to Wales 1867; died 1885.

Samuel, John: Born 1817, Swansea, S. Wales; glass-blower and Chartist (acc. to his friend, G. J. Holyoake). Left UK 1845 for Philadelphia, where he organized glass workers into union, 1857. Co-operative movements his chief concern in 1860's. Died 1909, Philadelphia.

Siney, John: Born 1830, Wigan, Lancs., cotton operative and brick-maker. Said later he had been 'a keen young Chartist', President, Wigan Brickmakers' Union, 1851–58; left UK 1863 for New York and St. Clair, Penn. Became first President, Miners' National Assoc. of the USA, 1873–76. Died 1880.

Smith, Joseph: Born 1798, Manchester, weaver, organizer for local group at Peterloo, 1819. Chartist 'courier' for Abel Heywood; left UK 1842 for Wissahicken, Pennsylvania, where he was 'a labour agitator'. (Yearley and Foner.) Died 1878.

Stephenson, Abel: Born 1805, Huddersfield, Yorks. Old clothes pedlar 'with a shop (cellar) in the town where meetings were held', Chartist who left UK 1839, 'dissatisfied with new Poor Law bill', bound for Pittsburgh and Northampton, Mass.

Stevens, John: Born 1825, Yeovil, moved to Trowbridge, house painter and decorator. Friend of Rev. Henry Solly, Secretary of Trowbridge National Charter Association, 1844; left UK 1847 bound for Philadelphia; 'Tales of an old Chartist' article in *Bizarre* magazine, signed J. S. could be his. (See *Bizarre*, Phil., vol. II, p. 355.)

Tinker, Christopher: Born 1797, Huddersfield, Yorks., bookseller/printer. Leading Owenite and later Chartist, author of *Crises* (Huddersfield, 1833), urged violence against Poor Law Commissioners in Huddersfield, January, 1837; left UK 1842 for Milwaukee, Wisc., settled in Spring Lake, Wisc., where he died, 1844. Visited by Pitkeithly?

Thompson, Mark: Born 1801, Newcastle-on-Tyne, Chartist, left UK 1840 for Troy, Penn. G. J. Harney corresponded with him in 1850's and stayed with him when he went to US 1863.

Thornton, William: Born Halifax, Yorks., Methodist preacher. Opened Chartist meeting at Peep Green, Whit Monday, 1839; 'physical force' friend and associate of O'Connor; left UK 1839, a 'wanted' man, for New York.

Trevellick, Richard: Born 1830, Scilly Isles, joiner and ship's carpenter in Southampton. Attended Chartist meetings with his uncle, active trade unionist; left UK 1852 bound for Melbourne, Australia, later went to US, arrived New Orleans, 1856; active in Eight Hours Movement and also in temperance, Brooklyn, 1862, Detroit, 1863; author of *Money and Panics* (Detroit, 1881), died 1895.

Trumbull, Matthew Mark: Born 1826, Westminster, London, moved to Deptford at age of three, bricklayer's labourer all over London and Home Counties ('on tramp'). Youthful Chartist, left UK 1846 for Montreal, 'tramped' to Boston, Mass., joined US army (Mexico), rose to sergeant, chased from Richmond, Va., for voicing Abolitionism, to Dubuque, Iowa, admitted to Iowa State Bar Association, 1858, pre-war friend of U. S. Grant, joined the army again 1860, rose to Brig.-Gen., wounded in action and semi-invalided, given political office in Iowa by President Grant; moved to Chicago to practice law; author of *Articles & Discussions on the Labor Question* (Chicago, 1890) with pseudonym, 'Wheelbarrow'; friend of Sam Fielden before Haymarket Riot, helped organize Amnesty Association afterwards, together with his German Socialist friend George Schilling, Henry Demarest Lloyd and Thomas Morgan; assistant editor, *The Open Court* magazine, 1886 to his death in 1894.

Vincent, Henry: Born 1810, Cheltenham. Chartist lecturer in Bristol and South Wales, arrested and imprisoned in Newport, Mon., 1839; very popular, and focal point of Newport Rising; left UK 1866 for New York, Philadelphia and Chicago, on lecture tour; went again 1868–70. Died in London, 1878.

Weaver, Daniel: Born 1824 in Staffordshire, coal miner. Chartist, departure from England, 1848, 'hastened by my political views'; went first to mines in Pennsylvania and then to Belleville, Ill., 1850; friend of Thomas Lloyd, and author of *What Might Be Done* (1860). Died 1899, in Illinois.

White, George: Born 1817, Bradford, Yorks., worked in and around Leeds, first as wool-comber, then as 'strong-arm' man for O'Connor. Reporter for *Northern Star*, though used more as a courier; left UK 1850, reported in Kansas City and California; returned to Leeds in 1860's. (See *Bradford Observer*, 18 Sept. 1869.)

Wolstenholme, John (or James): Born 1804, Dunfields, nr. Sheffield, Yorks., filemaker. Delegate to the first Chartist Convention, friend of G. Chatterton with whom he left UK, Sept. 1839, 'for America, with all their tools, to escape arrest' (*Sheffield Iris*, 1 Oct. 1839); reported in Westbury, Conn. Believed to have returned home 1850.

Wood, Duncan: Born 1810, London, pedlar/trader. Chartist, left UK 1842 for Boston, Mass., settled in Lawrence, Mass., as an emigrant's travel agent; prominent in Lawrence labour movement after Civil War.

Worswick, Benjamin: Born 1806, Clayton, Manchester; weaver and 'vigorous Chartist orator'. Associate of Peter Bussey; left UK 1840 for New York where he started a 'Chartist' boarding house (jointly with Bussey) in Front Street, 'close to the starting-point of the steamboats for the Western states'. Returned home in 1860's.

'Chartist children'

Cameron, Andrew Carr: Born 1834, Berwick-on-Tweed, son of a Chartist printer; became printer himself, left UK 1854 for Chicago, Ill., where became active in Typographical Union. Editor, *Workingman's Advocate*, 1864–80. Delegate to ILU in Basle, Switzerland, 1869. Died 1890 in Chicago, Ill.

Carnegie, Andrew: Born 1835, Dunfermline, Scot., son of Chartist William Carnegie; 'from bobbin-boy to steel magnate via telegraph boy'; left UK 1848 for Pittsburgh, Penn. Author of *Triumphant Democracy* (New York, 1886), returned to birthplace in 1886, launched a 'radical' newspaper in the town (which soon failed) and urged Scots to become Republican. Died 1919.

Fielden, Samuel: Born 1847, Todmorden, Lancs., son of Abraham Fielden (1816–86) who was principal spokesman for 'moral force'

Chartist group in Todmorden. Left UK 1868, worked as labourer in Boston, then to Chicago, Ill., when he had saved enough money to buy horse and cart and become a teamster; active in organizing teamsters' union; became friend of Albert Parsons, Socialist-Anarchist; and well-known Sunday afternoon stump-orator; arrested after Haymarket Riot, 1886, pardoned (after intervention of Amnesty Association) 1893. Died 1921.

Jarrett, John: Born 1843, Ebbw Vale, S. Wales, son of Chartist miner: an ironworker, he left UK 1861 for Duncansville and Harrisburg, Penn. Said he was converted to unionism by ex-Chartist, John Kane, while home in England 1867. Active union leader in Pennsylvania, 1870's.

Morgan, Thomas J.: Born 1847, Birmingham, son of a Chartist nail-maker; brassworker, 'in a place as near hell as one can conveniently get on this earth', from the age of nine; married 1868 and left UK 1869 for Chicago, Ill.; founder-president, Brassworkers' Independent Union, 1874; 'inspired to form an American Labor party' but dreams frustrated by Samuel Gompers; host (with H. D. Lloyd) to J. Keir Hardie, Aug. 1895. Died 1912. (See T. J. Morgan Papers, Univ. of Illinois.)

Phillips, Tom: Born 1833, Rotherham, Yorks., son of a Chartist shoemaker; had a shoemaker's shop in Sheffield till 1852 when left UK for New York, settled in Philadelphia, formed Union Co-operative Association No. I of Philadelphia, 1862; elected President of Boot and Shoe Workers' International Union, 1889. Died 1916.

The open court magazine (1887–1906)

An index of contributed articles in vols. I–XX used as research material, including authors, alphabetically arranged.

'Public Schools, What Shall they Teach?', M. M. Trumbull, VI, 3172.

'Scarcity making'. Wheelbarrow, II, 901.

'Schools, Industrial and Reform.' M. M. Trumbull, IV, 2638.

'Socialistic Scheme, A' (with remarks by M. M. Trumbull), VII, 3660.

'Strikes and Lockouts'. M. M. Trumbull, IV, 2611.

Trumbull, M. M. 'The Art of Making Poverty', I, 57, 97; 'Dilemma of a Double Allegiance', III, 1511; 'Henry George and Land Taxation', II, 1415; 'Jim the Investor', II, 1455; 'The Value of Doubt in the Study of History', I, 715; 'Words and Work', III, 1814, 'The Laokoon of Labor', I, 410; 'Live and not let Live', I, 261.

Trumbull, Gen. M. M., 'In Memoriam', by Paul Carus, VIII, 4145.

Trumbull, Gen. M. M., 'In Memoriam: The Farewell at the House', by Paul Carus, VIII, 4079. Also 4079, 4080, 4082, 4083, 4084, 4085 and 4086.

Waters, Amos. 'Individualism and Democracy in England', VI, 3511.

Bibliography

(I) Primary sources: books

Barker, Joseph. *The Life of Joseph Barker, written by himself*. Edited by J. T. Barker. London, 1880.

Bray, John Francis. *Labour's Wrongs and Labour's Remedy*. Leeds, 1838. —*A Voyage from Utopia*. Leeds, 1839. —*The Religion of Labour: God and Man A Unity, and All Mankind a Unity*. Chicago, 1879.

Brotherhead, William. *Forty Years Among the Old Booksellers of Philadelphia*. Philadelphia, 1891.

Brothers, Thomas. *The United States of North America as They Really Are: Not as They are Generally Described: Being a Cure for Radicalism*. London, 1840.

Brown, William. *America: Four Years' Residence in the United States and Canada*. Leeds, 1849.

Buckmaster, J. C. *A Village Politician: Life of John Buckley*. London, 1900.

Campbell, John. *A Theory of Equality: or the Way to Make Every Man Act Honestly*. Philadelphia, 1848. —*Negro-Mania*. Philadelphia, 1851.

Dealtry, William. *Money: Its History, Evils and Remedy*. Albany, 1858. —*The Laborer: A Remedy for his Wrongs*. Cincinnati, 1869.

Devyr, Thomas Ainge. *Our National Rights*. Belfast, 1836.—*The Odd Book, or Chivalry in Modern Days*. Greenpoint, New York, 1882.

Engels, Friedrich. *The Condition of the Working Class in England in 1844*. London, 1892.

Holyoake, George Jacob. *The Liberal Situation*. London, 1865. —*Sixty Years of an Agitator's Life*. London, 1893. —*Bygones Worth Remembering*. 2 vols. London, 1905. —*Among the Americans*. Chicago, 1881.

Johnston, David. *Autobiographical Reminiscences of David Johnston, an Octogenarian Scotchman*. Chicago, 1885.

Kydd, Samuel. *The History of the Factory Movement*. London, 1857.

Linton, W. J. *Threescore and Ten Years, 1820–90*. New York, 1894.

Lovett, William and Collins, J. *Chartism*. London, 1841.

Masquerier, Lewis. *Sociology or The Reconstruction of Society, Government and Property*. New York, 1877.

McNeill, George. *The Labor Movement*. Boston, 1887.

Prentice, Archibald. *A Tour in the United States*, London, 1848.

Rose, J. H. *The Rise of Democracy*. London, 1897.

Solly, Henry. *James Woodford, Carpenter and Chartist*. London, 1881.

Trumbull, Matthew Mark. *The Trial of the Judgement, A Review of the Anarchist Case*. Chicago, 1888. —'Wheelbarrow', *Articles on the Labor Question*. Chicago, 1890. —*The Free Trade Struggle in England*. Chicago, 1892.

Wilson, Benjamin. *The Struggles of an Old Chartist*. Halifax, 1887.

(II) Primary sources: newspapers, pamphlets and periodicals

Bray, John Francis. *American Destiny—What Shall it be, Republican or Cossack, An Argument Addressed to the People of the Late Union*. New York, 1864.

Cassen, Herbert. 'The English in America', *Munsey's Magazine*, XXXV, New York, 1906.

Linton, J. W. 'Who were the Chartists?', *Century Magazine*, Jan., 1882, New York.

Ludlow, J. M. 'Some of the Christian Socialists of 1848 and the Following Years', *Economic Review*, Jan., 1894.

Smyles, Dr. John. '*A letter to Mr. Pitkethly*', London, 1842.

The Open Court. See Appendix B.

The Athenaeum, 2, June 1894. No. 3475, p. 713 (Trumbull obituary).

The Bee-Hive, 1860–65.

Blackwood's Magazine, 1825–37.

Bronterre's National Reformer.

Carpenter's Political Letters.

Chartist Circular.

Manchester Guardian.

McDouall's Chartist Journal.

Newcastle Weekly Chronicle.

Northern Star.

Notes to the People.

Pioneer.

Poor Man's Guardian.

Sheffield Iris.

The Charter, 1839–40.

The Times.

(III) Secondary sources: books

Armytage, W. H. G. *Heavens Below*. Oxford, 1961. —*A. J. Mundella, 1825–1897*. London, 1951.

Aron, Raymond. *Main Currents in Sociological Thought*. New York, 1965.

Athearn, R. G. *Westward the Briton*. New York, 1953.

Berthoff, Rowland T. *British Immigrants in Industrial America, 1790–1950*. Harvard, 1953.

Billington, Ray. *Westward Expansion*. New York, 1960,

Carrothers, W. A. *Emigration from the British Isles*. London, 1929.

Christman, Henry. *Tin Horns and Calico*. New York, 1945.

Clark, G. Kitson. *The Making of Victorian England*. London, 1950.

Cole, Donald B. *Immigrant City*. University of North Carolina, 1963.

Cole, G. D. H. *Chartist Portraits*. London, 1941.

Copeland, M. T. *The Cotton Manufacturing Industry of the United States*. Cambridge (Mass.), 1912.

Cross, Whitney R. *The Burned-Over District*. Cornell, 1950.

David, Henry. *The History of the Haymarket Affair*. New York, 1963.

Dorfman, Joseph. *The Economic Mind in American Civilization, 1606–1865*. Vol. 2. New York, 1946.

Duncan, William. *Life of Joseph Cowen*. London, 1904.

Foner, Philip S. *History of the Labor Movement in the United States*. Vol. I. New York, 1947.

Ginger, Ray. *Altgeld's America*. New York, 1958.

Hansen, Marcus. *The Immigrant in American History*. Harvard, 1948.

Harrison, Royden. *Before the Socialists*. London, 1965.

Hovell, Mark. *The Chartist Movement*. Manchester, 1918. (3rd Ed. 1966).

Lillibridge, George Donald. *Beacon of Freedom. The Impact of American Democracy upon Great Britain 1830–1870*. Philadelphia, 1955.

Read, Donald and Glasgow, E. *Feargus O'Connor*. London, 1961.

Saville, J. *Ernest Jones: Chartist*. London, 1952.

Schluter, H. *Lincoln, Labor and Slavery*. New York, 1913.

Schoyen, A. R. *The Chartist Challenge*. New York, 1958.

Shepperson, Wilbur Stanley. *British Emigration to North America*. Oxford, 1957. —*Emigration and Disenchantment*. Oklahoma, 1965.

Thistlethwaite, Frank. *The Anglo-American Connection in the Early Nineteenth Century*. Philadelphia, 1959.

Thompson, E. P. *The Making of the English Working Class*. London, 1963.

Van der Zee, Jacob. *The British In Iowa*. Iowa, 1922.

Vincent, John. *The Formation of the Liberal Party*. London, 1966.

West, Julius. *A History of the Chartist Movement*. London, 1920.

Williams, David. *John Frost, a study in Chartism*. Cardiff, 1939.

Wright, Leslie C. *Scottish Chartism*. London, 1953.

Yearley, Clifton K. Jr. *Britons in American Labor. A History of the Influence of the United Kingdom Immigrants on American Labor, 1820–1914*. Baltimore, 1957.

Zahler, Helene Sara. *Eastern Workingmen and National Land Policy, 1829–1862*. New York, 1941

(IV) Secondary sources: articles and periodicals

Brook, Michael. 'Joseph Barker and *The People*, the True Emigrant's Guide', *Publications of the Thoresby Society*, XLVI (1957–61), 331–78.

Faulkner, H. U. 'Chartism and the Churches', *Columbia University Studies in History, Economics and Public Law*, LXXIII (1916), 469–616.

Harrison, Brian. 'Chartism, Liberalism and the Life of R. Lowery', *English Historical Review*, July, 1967.

Harrison, J. F. C. 'Chartism in Leeds', *Chartist Studies* (Asa Briggs, ed.), London, 1959.

O'Higgins, Rachel. 'The Irish Influence on the Chartist Movement', *Past and Present*, Vol. XX, Nov., 1961, 84–85.

Pessen, Edward. 'Thomas Brothers, Anti-Capitalist Employer', *Pennsylvania History*, XXIV, Oct., 1957, 323–26.

Rezneck, Samuel. 'The Social History of an American Depression, 1837–1843', *American Historical Review*, Vol. 40, 662–87.

Wall, J. F. 'Andrew Carnegie: Child of Chartism', *History 4* (a Meridian periodical, published by World Pub. Co.), 1961.

Index